THE INTERNET IS
MY RELIGION

THE INTERNET IS MY RELIGION

JIM GILLIAM

WITH LEA ENDRES

NATIONBUILDER

LOS ANGELES

NationBuilder
520 S. Grand Avenue, Second Floor
Los Angeles, CA 90071

Library of Congress Control Number: 2015937871

Designed by Jonathan D. Lippincott

nationbuilder.com

1   3   5   7   9   10   8   6   4   2

For Mom

CONTENTS

FOREWORD

Are great leaders born or made? As someone who invests in and advises CEOs, I care deeply about that question. Do great leaders come out of the womb with the charisma, grit, and courage to move men and women to do great things? Or are great leaders forged from intense experience and great training? There are many seemingly "natural" leaders, but almost none would say that they were born that way. But if leaders are made, then why is true leadership nearly impossible to teach?

I was never really comfortable with my answer to this question until I met Jim Gilliam. I first met Jim when he came to pitch my venture capital firm Andreessen Horowitz to invest in his company NationBuilder. NationBuilder,

Jim explained, was software that he built to help leaders communicate with and organize their followers. It was a breakthrough concept made possible by a series of prior technological advances, including the development of the internet and the rise of social networking.

As interesting as NationBuilder was, it still had what we affectionately refer to in technology as "a bootstrapping problem." Bootstrapping, taken from the nineteenth-century-era phrase, refers to starting a self-sustaining process. For example, how do you start a computer before loading the operating system into memory? You need a process before the process. Leadership software was great, but where would the leaders come from?

To understand the solution to NationBuilder's bootstrapping problem, I first had to understand Jim.

Exceptionally tall, impossibly thin, and white as ghost, Jim does not look like a born leader. His shy personality and awkward manner only reinforce this initial perception. Beyond that, Jim has no military or management training. He has not worked for great leaders in his career, and he has no formal training.

Yet Jim is a real leader. He has a clear, compelling vision, he inspires people to greatness, and he leads with a focus so intense that if you get in his way, he'll burn a hole in you with his eyes. He had already accomplished amazing things in life, ranging from turning obscure documentary films into blockbusters to rallying a community that he created to help him get a new pair of lungs after chemotherapy had burned out his original pair. And then, with no background and no connections, he built a very promising new company.

If Jim was neither born nor made, where did this come from? How did this gangly, awkward man learn to lead?

As I got to know Jim and his story, I learned the answer to this question and to my larger question as well. Leaders are neither born nor made; they are found. This book is about Jim's journey to find his inner leader. It's a journey that all leaders must go through, but one that almost nobody ever talks about. It's about learning to think for yourself and sharing what you know in the best and most impactful way possible. I hope that as you read this book, you will find your inner leader—and then lead the world to great things.

Ben Horowitz
March 2015

THE INTERNET IS
MY RELIGION

INTRODUCTION

I'd just flown into New York. I was staying at a random stranger's apartment near NYU that I'd found through Airbnb after Facebook informed me that we had three mutual friends. The wi-fi password was not on a sticky note in the kitchen like it was supposed to be. I texted the owner, but she didn't know what the password was. Why was this not a big deal? If the water wasn't working, that would be a crisis, but I could do without a shower before I could do without internet!

I was a little high strung. Crazy nervous, really. In two days I would be giving the most important speech of my life. Standing in front of 800 of the most influential political and technology professionals in the world, I was going to tell a deeply personal story about religion that I wasn't even sure I could get through without crying. I had no idea how they would react, and I was terrified that I'd be booed off the stage.

The morning of the Personal Democracy Forum, I sat between Ben Rattray from Change.org and Jay Rosen from NYU in the first row as I waited for my turn to speak. It felt like I was the only person in the entire room not staring at a glowing screen. Instead, I was staring at the floor reciting the speech over and over again in my head. Then three friends—Lea, Ramin, and Jesse—walked in and sat behind me. They were the only ones who knew what I was about to do.

Micah Sifry, the conference organizer and a great friend, called me to the stage. I repeated the first line of the speech in my head, *Growing up I had two loves: Jesus and the internet.* And then I started.

In the Christian faith, giving one's testimony about how Jesus saved your life is the necessary rite of passage. It's the personal story of transformation that spreads the Good News from person to person, one by one, to every corner of the earth. These stories of faith in Christ formed the basis for the infrastructure behind the most powerful movement in human history. So on that day, I shared my struggle with faith, my story of transformation, my testimony—with a twist.

Towards the end, people started clapping. I waited, but then everyone kept clapping and started standing up! It was the last thing I expected. I finally got my head together and motioned that I had one more thing to say, just one more thing.

When I finished, the place erupted again. I had managed not to cry, just barely. But, looking around the room, it seemed like others hadn't. Completely exhausted, totally overwhelmed, and fully unable to process what was happening, I snuck out through the side entrance of the auditorium. A couple people from the audience ran after me. More people kept coming, but my friends finally found me and steered me away. Alone, we stared at each other in disbelief.

"What just happened?!"

"Um . . . I think you just started a religion."

"Oh my God, I forgot this was being livestreamed."

And then Ramin asked, "Did you see Twitter?" That got everyone's attention.

There were *thousands* of tweets.

Within a couple days, the video had been seen 300,000 times and I had a major publisher offer me a $100,000 book deal. Agents were crawling all over me. They told me I could sell my story for a million dollars if I wanted and there would be a hundred copies in every bookstore.

But what no one knew was that Lea and I had been working on a book for over a year. It was through that process with her that I'd come to discover what I really believed, and why I knew—and knew I had to tell—my story.

I was an activist and a geek. I saw my strength as building technology infrastructure for leaders and had just started a new company, NationBuilder, to do exactly that. But I'd learned about the power of stories while producing documentaries. The stories we tell create our culture. They illuminate our worldviews. It took me a long time to accept that possibly the most important thing I could offer wasn't something I would build, but was simply telling my story.

I believe that there is a new worldview. One based on internet values and the connectedness of all humanity—where instead of waiting for a savior, we create the future. And I now know that I'm not the only one who feels this way.

I turned down the book deals and told the agents to go away. We're publishing this on the internet, for free. For this story, there really is no other way. I have faith that you will share it with your friends, family, and community— that's the only way it will exist in the world. But most importantly, I hope that you will share your own story, your testimony, your faith in what's possible when God just happens.

INFINITY'S EDGE

In the beginning was the personal computer.

I was thirteen months old when my parents moved from Southern California to Woodstock, New York, so my dad could realize his lifelong dream of working for IBM, the world's then-largest computer company. It was 1978, a year after the release of the Apple II, and the beginning of what would become the personal-computer revolution.

Two years later, IBM announced its answer to Apple and the other personal computers that were becoming popular with hobbyists—the IBM PC. A year from the PC's release, there was just one small problem: IBM didn't have any software for it. The PC would be useless to the average person without software, so the

PC division launched the Employee Software Program, which gave employees the opportunity to create and submit software and, if the software was accepted by IBM, to receive royalties on each copy of it that was sold. It was every computer geek's dream. The PC specs were distributed internally and ideas began flying around. Like everyone else, my dad was desperate to get his hands on an actual computer, but the employee waiting list was excruciatingly long. Finally, in November 1981, he got the call that his computer was ready.

This was my big chance. To avoid paying New York sales tax on the five-thousand-dollar computer, my dad had ordered it from a store in Nashua, New Hampshire, two hundred miles away. Which meant that Dad was going on a road trip. And, as a four-year-old who had to stay at home with my mom every day, nothing was more exciting to me than the possibility of going on an adventure with my dad. I begged him to let me come along, and when I was finally sitting by his side in his cool brown Ford Pinto, I was in heaven. Four hours later, my dad put down the seat in the hatchback and heaved two gigantic boxes into the back. I wasn't sure what they contained, but I knew it had to be something special.

Computers of the era were mainframes—giant multiuser machines that were housed in their own rooms and accessible only to trained operators. Each computer cycle was precious, and they were allocated judiciously only to the most deserving. These mainframes were real computers, and real computers were IBM's business. The hobbyist desire for a personal computer had required a response, but IBM assumed that because the PC could be used by only one person at a time, it would never have enough power to do more than one thing at a time. It was a throw-away machine, as evidenced by the nonchalance with which the Employee Software Program was launched. No one expected it to be more than a silly little crap computer. Except for my dad and his buddy Larry Raper.

My dad worked on his new computer all the time. I sat next to him, keeping as quiet as I could as he pounded the keys of the magical machine. The clickety-clack of the keyboard echoed through the house, always drawing me back beside him. My mom and my baby sister, Kelly, happily ignored us. Cryptic-looking characters appeared on the screen as my dad typed, and I just knew that he was doing something important. What I didn't know was that he was working on his opus—an operating system called Program Manager that would allow the PC to multitask. No one at the company thought such a thing was possible, so for the next six months my dad and Larry worked every night and through the weekends to prove them wrong. In June 1982, they started beta testing Program Manager with their fellow employees, and it stunned all of IBM. What they'd accomplished was inconceivable, and my dad spent the next six months taking trips to the PC division in Boca Raton, Florida, to explain how it worked.

By the end of the year, the higher-ups in the company understood that with Program Manager, IBM had an operating system that wouldn't have to be licensed from outside the company. IBM would own it outright and could ship it with every computer. Beyond. Epic. My dad and Larry signed a contract with Don Estridge, the head of the PC division, which included an eleven-dollar-per-copy royalty agreement and a job for my dad at IBM

Research out in Silicon Valley. They had done the impossible.

Team Gilliam was on fire. Right around that time, my mom gave birth to my new baby sister, Kristen; we bought a fancy house in San Jose, California; and Mom, the girls, and I headed west while Dad stayed in Woodstock to pack up our house. The night before the movers were scheduled to come, Larry called. The deal was off; without any explanation, IBM was killing Program Manager.

My dad was beside himself. We'd already sold our house and bought a new one with a massive mortgage; the family was waiting in California, and if my dad left IBM he'd have to pay back all the moving expenses, which he couldn't afford to do. But most importantly, he needed to know what had happened. Why would IBM turn its back on such an important technology?

My dad and Larry kept pushing for an explanation but they got none, so they flew to Boca Raton to see Don Estridge in person. He kept trying to appease them with corporate speak, but my dad wouldn't let him off the hook. Finally, Don said that to launch the PC on time, IBM had made a contract to ship a software called DOS—what everyone considered to be a weak operating system, and that IBM would not own—with every computer. It hadn't expected to have its own operating system, let alone one far superior to everything else on the market, and designed specifically for the IBM PC. But IBM had already committed to DOS, and it didn't want to hurt its relationship with the new guy on the scene, Bill Gates, or his company, Microsoft.

Furious, my dad knew that with their signed contract, he and Larry could sue IBM. So they met with IBM's chief legal counsel, Nicholas Katzenbach, who had previously served as attorney general under President Lyndon B. Johnson. Katzenbach made one thing clear: IBM owned them. They could try battling Goliath, but they would most certainly lose, and the whole ordeal would be hell for them and their families, both financially and emotionally. My dad wanted to fight; Larry didn't. IBM offered a settlement of $40,000. To prevent my dad from quitting and going to work for a competitor, the company spread out the payments over three years. And they each got a new PC . . . with DOS.

Historically, that moment was important,

given what happened as a result—Microsoft slaughtered IBM in the software business and Bill Gates became the richest man in the world—but for our family it just meant that we became Christian fundamentalists.

The Moral Majority and Me

I don't remember falling off the jungle gym. It was my favorite place to be at recess, high atop the playground and away from all the screaming kids. I knew everyone expected me to make friends at my new school, but I just wanted to read my book. Alice gave me access to a different world filled with strange characters and endless adventures. Wonderland came alive every night in my dreams, where I was chased by the Queen through winding mazes. I built castles in the sandbox, but when others came to play with me, I escaped to the top of the jungle gym. There I perched, reading, lost in my own daydreams. Then one day I fell. And unlike Alice after her fall, I was actually hurt. I needed stitches. But the cool part was that my copy of *Alice in Wonderland* was forever after covered in blood.

Every day after school, I'd rush home for a very important date: to watch Penny and Brain secretly save the day on *Inspector Gadget*. Our new home in Silicon Valley was nothing like our house in Woodstock. On Dorsey Lane there was no lake that would freeze over in the winter, no deer eating the vegetables in our garden, no giant woodpile in front of our house. We were in a new suburban tract home, not in the middle of nowhere, and I could now visit our neighbors without climbing a huge hill. And instead of a forest at the edge of our backyard, we now had Los Gatos Christian Church.

My parents rarely went to church when we lived in New York, so I'd never really been to one before. Even if I had, it wouldn't have been anything like Los Gatos Christian Church. LGCC was not your average congregation. It was one of the country's new megachurches, and it was ground zero for the growing fundamentalist movement in the United States—and for Jerry Falwell's newly established Moral Majority. When we walked in for our first Sunday service, we were welcomed by thousands of members; a choir of singers who all could have had recording contracts; and information about the youth basketball, baseball, and soccer leagues. The church bulletin announced that fall enrollment was open for the elementary and middle schools. My parents were impressed.

Christianity had always been a part of their lives. My mom was raised a Christian and my dad became one in junior high because, as my mom liked to tease him, all the pretty girls were in Sunday school. They both attended First Baptist Church of Downey throughout high school, but it wasn't until a summer night in 1971 that they finally met. My dad was on break from University of California, Irvine, and decided to go to his first evening service in years. My mom decided to do the same thing on the same June night. When you're in college there's always an after-party—even after church. When they bumped into each other there, my mom recognized my dad as the guy who used to play guitar and lead the songs in their high school youth group. She'd just returned home from a vacation, was exhausted, and felt gross. My dad was instantly smitten.

There was something special about Kathy. She was undeniably beautiful, but what hooked my dad was that she was a math major at University of California, Los Angeles. Rather than asking her how old she was, he asked which math classes she was taking. Recognizing all the upper-division classes she had listed, he figured out that she was going into her senior year. Kathy thought his tactic was pretty clever, so she said yes when he asked her to a beach party the following day. He picked her up the next afternoon in his spotless red Camaro, which was not nearly as impressive to her as his math skills were. Over the next few months, driving back and forth between Irvine and L.A., my dad learned that Kathy was fiercely moral, creative, and crazy smart—and that she refused to listen to the people who said that "good girls" should just study social sciences. She was a math geek, the only woman in most of her classes, and intent on getting her teaching certificate so she could teach high-school students. And, for some reason, she thought my dad's pi jokes were charming. Q.E.D. They were married nine months later and within a few years were happily raising a family. Their love was the pillar of our lives; Christianity was just part of the scenery.

My dad was the one who changed that. He'd done everything the "right" way. He'd gone to college, worked hard, had a family, and gotten his dream job with the one company he believed was going to change the world. But

IBM had shunned his software out of coward-ice. He suddenly found himself bound with shiny golden handcuffs to a company he had no faith in. My dad lost his purpose, and in the wake of his devastation, my parents fell head-first into Los Gatos Christian Church and its ready-made community.

It was LGCC's assistant pastor Mike Williams who radicalized him. Mike was teaching from John MacArthur's *The Gospel According to Jesus*, and he insisted my dad read it. The book's main premise was that many people who think that they are Christian really aren't. You had to choose: Were you going to be a lip-service Christian who shows up only on Sundays, or were you going to dedicate your life to the service of Jesus? My parents chose. They went all in.

For the next few years, I existed completely in the insular, protective, perfectly curated fundamentalist-Christian bubble that my parents created for me. I went to school, played piano, and went to church, all within a one-mile radius. My dad coached all my sports teams in the church's leagues. My parents held monthly small-group Bible studies at our home. There was no part of my life that wasn't church, which was fine with me, because church was exciting. On some Sundays we even had to drive through people yelling at us in order to get to the service. Apparently, we were very popular.

But that was nothing like when the preacher from TV came to town. It was May 7, 1986, and I was actually going to get to see Jerry Falwell in person. My parents and I regularly watched his *Old Time Gospel Hour*, and my dad had even donated enough money to get his own special printing of the *Old Time Gospel Hour Bible*. My mom kept it next to the TV in the family room. On the short drive to the church, we passed hundreds of protesters—all yelling and shaking signs at us. I had no idea what they were saying, but it was intoxicating. I was part of something that all these people cared about! The sermon was electric. Dr. Jerry Falwell rallied the crowd with the Moral Majority's past victories—including the election of Ronald Reagan to the presidency in 1980—and with the victories still to come. I had no idea what abortion or the "gay plague" was, but I knew one thing: this was the place to be.

A few months later, I was born again. Many Christians baptize infants, but in the Protestant faith, you have to make the decision to let Jesus into your heart yourself to receive His grace. I hadn't yet, but all my friends at church had, my teachers wanted me to, and I knew it would make my parents proud. As my dad put me to bed one night I told him that I wanted Jesus to come into my heart. I wanted his grace to wash away my sins. What did I have to do? My dad said that all I had to do was say a special prayer. He told me to repeat after him, "Dear Jesus. I believe you are the son of God, you died on the cross for my sins, and rose from the dead three days later. Please forgive me of my sins, and come into my heart to be my Lord and Savior. Thank you Jesus. Amen."

After I finished the prayer, I went to the bathroom to brush my teeth. I looked at myself in the mirror and smiled. My dad asked me if I looked different. I said that I did. Of course I did—I was giving my life to Jesus. All I had to do now was declare it to my church and be publicly baptized.

At the end of the morning service the following Sunday, I walked to the front of the auditorium with my parents and told the deacon I was ready to be baptized. He took me to a special room and asked for my testimony. I told him how much I loved Jesus and that

I believed he was my Savior. He smiled, held my hand while we prayed together, then pulled out the master calendar. Because there were so many people accepting Jesus into their hearts at LGCC, baptisms had to be prescheduled. He slotted me in for three weeks later.

At Los Gatos Christian Church, baptisms were a public spectacle. The church auditorium seated three thousand and the stage made for an impressive show. It was flanked on the right by a screen showing song lyrics and on the left by the baptismal pool. Above everything hung a massive, backlit cross. Those being reborn did so with full theater lighting and an audience of thousands. I was terrified. I was shy and hated being noticed. But this wasn't about me. It was about Jesus.

On the evening of my baptism, Dad dropped me off backstage and a church deacon gave me a white robe. I changed in the bathroom and then headed, trembling, to the waiting area. When it was time, the pastor called me out onto the platform. Standing in my robe before the pool, I was introduced to the congregation as a member making a public stand for Jesus. The eyes of thousands of fellow believers bore witness as I was dipped in the water three times, signifying my rebirth into the body of Christ "in the name of the Father, the Son, and the Holy Spirit." I was eight years old.

For the next two years, I was killing it with Jesus. I was the star of my baseball team, I had a ton of friends, I rocked my piano lessons, and I dominated the playground with my four-square skills. Little did I know that at the same time, my parents were listening to Dr. Falwell trash the West Coast, and California was beginning to look to them like heathen territory—especially to my mom. She wanted to raise her children in a more godly environment. My parents broke the news that we were moving the summer before I turned ten. My dad was transferring to IBM's facility at the Research Triangle Park in North Carolina. Leaving Los Gatos made no sense to me, and I didn't want to go, but my parents assured me that we'd find a similar community wherever we went. And they were right: I did find a community. But it was nothing like LGCC.

Rush Limbaugh vs. Tori Amos

We moved to Chandler's Green, a brand-new subdivision that had been carved out of a forest between Chapel Hill and Durham. Our huge house was surrounded by towering pines, and I liked to stay up late and watch the Carolina rainstorms turn the trees into dancing giants. There was only one other boy in the neighborhood when we moved in, so I ended up playing a lot of basketball with my dad. But the biggest difference in my life was the reappearance of my dad's computer. I hadn't seen it since we'd left Woodstock, but when we arrived in Chapel Hill, he put it upstairs in the family room where we all watched TV. I started to sit next to him again, pestering him with questions while he worked on the computer.

One day he brought home a funny-looking phone thing that plugged in to his computer. When I asked my dad what it was, he told me that it was a modem, and that it connected the computer in our family room to his computer at work. I watched in disbelief as he punched commands into his home computer that would then control the computer at his office. Wait, what? Computers could talk to each other?! What were they saying? What was on all the other computers? My dad didn't have the answers, but I had to know. I became curiouser and curiouser, and I was determined to figure out how to connect our computer to all the other computers.

I begged my mom to take me to the library so I could scour books and magazines for the answers. But all the computer magazines were just about computers and not about modems! So I went to the stacks where they had old, un-indexed magazines and combed through them, looking for any clue that might tell me what to do next. I finally hit the gold mine and dis-covered that our modem was 1200 bps—and that I needed special software called ProComm to use it. By some miracle, ProComm didn't cost a thing; I just had to pay for the diskette that it came on. When the disk arrived a few weeks later, I immediately loaded the software on my dad's computer. Now all I had to do was find a phone number that actually had a com-puter on the other end of it. There was only one thing that could help me on my quest, so I begged my mom to take me to the local drug-store. There I found *Computer Shopper*—every computer geek's Bible—sitting right next to all the trashy romance novels. But *Computer Shop-per* was no ordinary magazine. It was two arti-cles and a thousand pages of mail-order ads for everything a computer lover could ever want. Plus the one thing I was looking for: tiny classified listings of Bulletin Board Systems (BB-Ses)—computers to call in every area code in the country.

Even though we lived in Chapel Hill, we had a Durham phone number, so that was the only area code I could call for free. I scanned through hundreds of listings until I found one for Durham. I scribbled Bull City BBS's number on my hand, carefully concealing it from my mom as she drove me home. I raced upstairs, loaded up ProComm, and held my breath as I dialed the number. The modem made the most bizarre squealing sound I'd ever heard, like it was trying to mate with a rhinoceros. It was the sound I would hear for many years, the sound that meant computers were talking to each other. I stared at the screen, waiting for something to happen—please God, please God!—then miraculously, line by line, text began to appear. The only thing that prevented me from jumping around the room was fear of missing what was going to happen next.

When the screen finished loading I saw what every boy who's been forbidden to play Nintendo dreams of: free games. Lots of free games. I gorged myself for a few weeks before I got bored. I started poking around and found listings for a few other Durham BBSes, and saw that BBSes weren't just about games or software; they were a whole other world. Each BBS was a community with its own culture. And the best part? It didn't matter what I looked like or how old I was.

When you're twelve years old, you don't want to stand out. And I literally stood out. I was 6'2". But online I didn't have to slouch. No one knew I was tall or geeky or awkward. They didn't know that I had skipped seventh grade and was the youngest kid in my class. I got to hang out with people way older than me, and they took me seriously. BBSes were the place to be. They were almost as exciting as right-wing talk radio.

Rush Limbaugh had only recently exploded onto the national scene, and my dad was a full-on dittohead. Rush made liberal-bashing a sport. We were building a movement mocking feminazis and tree huggers, and my young skull full of mush couldn't get enough of it. I listened to him every afternoon, along with WRTP Durham—a 10,000-watt AM station that was a combination of contemporary Christian music and conservative talk radio. It was the perfect station for me because they fused God and country together, just like Los Gatos. And it was small enough that I could make my favorite songs number one on the weekly countdown by calling in over and over again.

Soon, I was a regular caller on Adam McManus's "Take A Stand" program. I called in on Earth Day and trashed the environmental movement, faithfully reciting Rush's talking points. Adam was so impressed that he invited me to come to the station and find out how it all worked. The first thing I saw when I walked in was that he had not one but two CD players! He showed me everything—all the records, how you can speed up or slow down songs to make them fit in the allotted time, and that he just dialed the weather number every hour so he could report it to his listeners. All the mystery disappeared from my beloved radio program; it was just one person taking a stand and having an impact. I could do that for what I cared about, too! And there was just one thing that really mattered to everyone I knew: the murder of four thousand unborn babies every day.

I'd been hearing about the horrors of abortion for years, and it was time for me to do something about it. My parents didn't think that a trip to the annual March for Life rally in Washington, D.C.—commemorating the anniversary of the Supreme Court's *Roe v. Wade* decision—would make for much of a family vacation, so I convinced them to put a bumper sticker on our car that said, THE MOST DANGEROUS PLACE TO LIVE IN AMERICA IS IN A MOTHER'S WOMB. The sticker caused a lot of grief in our neighborhood, and resulted in a few notes—which said things like "the most dangerous place to live in America is in YOUR mind"—being left on our car, but I was undeterred. I had to take a stand, just like Adam and Rush. I passed out flyers on the Fourth of July. I made comparisons to the Holocaust and the Vietnam and Korean Wars, righteously indignant that this injustice was occurring in our country every single day.

Meanwhile, my mom was growing frustrated with my education. After graduating from UCLA with her math degree, she'd gotten her teaching certificate as planned, then taught algebra to rival gang members at Los Angeles High School. After five years she left to raise me, and she poured all her energy into ensuring that I received the best education possible. In Woodstock, it was at the well-regarded Montessori school. In California, it was LGCC. But in North Carolina it was the tiny Cresset Christian Academy, and CCA just wasn't cutting it.

She knew I wasn't being challenged, but when she found out that my math teacher was making me sit off to the side and teach myself with a different textbook than all the other kids were using, it was the last straw. One day I came home from school and my parents told me I never had to go back. We were moving to Raleigh, where they'd found a more Bible-believing church, and my mom was going to teach us herself. That was fine by me. Raleigh had a lot more BBSes.

To Mom, being our teacher was a serious duty, and it gave her the opportunity to fully shield us from the corrupting influences of the secular world. Now parent, teacher, and moral guide, my mom was on a mission to create the perfect children. She taught my sisters at the kitchen table every day, but because I was older, my lessons were assigned in the morning and then reviewed by my dad when he got home from work. This new system worked out perfectly for me, because I was pretty much on my own during the day. All I had to do was plow through my schoolwork, and then I could focus on my real mission: building an intergalactic empire. Trade Wars was my new favorite game. There weren't any graphics, but that didn't matter, because you didn't play against the computer—you played online, against other real people! Methodically exploring trade routes and plotting universal domination was way more interesting than cell mitosis.

Right after my thirteenth birthday, my dad inadvertently shoved me further down the rabbit hole. New versions of PCs were popping up everywhere, and he decided that it was finally time to get a faster computer. It was a huge purchase, and I pored over copies of *Computer Shopper*, trying to figure out what model he should buy. We ended up committing sacrilege and deliberately got an IBM clone instead of an IBM. But our act of rebellion didn't matter much in the end. His computer was one of the first models to have Windows, the new program Microsoft had created to enable the PC to multitask. When you turned on the computer, the first thing that appeared was the name of that program. It was called Program Manager.

My dad gave me the old computer, but I used his all the time because I needed a faster computer to crush my new favorite game, Sim-City. In most games, winning meant killing someone or destroying something. But Sim-City was about building. I learned about urban planning and how systems worked. Then I learned the secret to winning: what really mattered was what the programmer thought was the right way to do something. I could reduce pollution and make my city more attractive to residents by building only train stations. Who needs cars anyway? It was totally impractical, but it didn't matter, because I was living in the world created by the programmer. The SimCity programmer was God, and understanding what God wanted helped me build better cities and make my citizens happy.

The more I played the game, the further I fell into the SimCity community. My dad's computer had Prodigy, a precursor to America Online. The creators of Prodigy thought their service would be used for shopping, and email would be used primarily to send customers their sales receipts, but I used it to connect with other SimCity players. We figured out how to send email to a large group of people all at once, and we formed an unofficial Sim-City Club. Together we learned how to hack the game, cram as many people as possible into our towns while minimizing pollution—hint, no roads!—and share our cities. We weren't the only ones to figure out this mailing-list trick, and soon Prodigy started charging people to send email. This completely shut down our club, as sending a single message would have cost over forty dollars, but it devastated the Prodigy community as a whole, too. It was like the barista walking around the coffee shop demanding a quarter before you could talk to your friends. It was outrageous. Thousands of people protested. But it didn't matter, because Prodigy only cared about people communicating with one another if they could make money from it. So I decided that I would build a space for people to hang out—I was going to start my own BBS.

There were just two things standing in my way. First, my computer was way too slow to run a BBS, and, second, I needed a separate, dedicated phone line. I didn't think I could sell either of those ideas to my parents. But an unforeseen variable soon came to my aid: my dad's love for my mom. She was burning out on teaching my sisters, so he wrote a custom program to automate half of the day's lessons. He converted the Bob Jones homeschooling textbooks into a database of questions that my sisters and I would have to answer with exactly the correct responses, letter for letter. They were called our "files," and my parents realized that all three of us kids would only be able to do them at the same time if we had our own computers. So they bought two for my sisters, and I convinced my dad that it would be cheaper if he gave me his—which just happened to be a lot faster. He said yes. A few months later, my parents got so sick of me tying up the home phone line that they got another one. I had everything I needed for my BBS. :)

A few weeks later, I unveiled with great pride . . . Gilligan's Island. The afternoon of the launch, my eyes were fixed on the screen, waiting for my first caller. But by dinnertime no one had dialed in, and I was deflated. What if people didn't want to be a part of my community? I connected a phone to the modem so I would hear if a call came in during dinner. After two bites of poached chicken and quinoa, the phone rang and I bolted upstairs to watch my first user. After scoping the place out, he posted a public message welcoming me and my new board to the scene. Holy crap! That was it for me, I was hooked. I'd built something that mattered, and I never wanted to do anything else ever again. I spent all my time designing and coding my online space. Eventually, the phone would ring so often that I had to turn off the ringer.

Then the unthinkable happened. One Sunday afternoon, I came home from church and discovered that someone had hacked Gilligan's Island. I was mortified, but no one was going to stop me. I immediately started designing a new BBS—Infinity's Edge. This time I was much smarter and more cynical in how I built it. My second week online, someone called into Infinity's Edge as "Doppelganger." The person requested a chat with the sysop—me—and we started chatting. "Doppelganger" became an online friend, but after a while Andy (his real name) and I began talking on the phone. It turned out his dad also worked for IBM. We traded ideas back and forth for weeks, until he revealed to me that he was the one who'd hacked my BBS—which made us even better friends.

Andy was definitely not a Christian. While

I'd been teaching at Vacation Bible School, attending Bob Jones University's Homeschool Conferences with my parents, and going on mission trips, he'd been working at a record store and calling pirate BBSes. He introduced me to an edgier side of the online world, even as I relentlessly tried to convert him. Andy and I figured out how to get on the internet—this thing we'd heard about that connected all the important computers in the world. He set up his computer to war dial thousands of phone numbers and to keep track of any computers that answered. Then we called each one to see if it was a university or a corporate network that was connected to the internet. Once connected, we used telnet to connect to any computer we wanted, for free. We were moving up in the world.

But to be really cool, I needed a faster modem. All the elites had fast modems and they wouldn't waste their time calling BBSes with slow ones. My social status was in jeopardy. I needed a 14.4k modem from USRobotics, the online equivalent of a Ferrari. The problem, of course, was my parents. They were completely in charge of my money; anything I had ever earned and saved was in their possession, logged meticulously in a little red book known as "the card." So, even once I had saved up enough money, I would still have to convince my parents to let me buy the modem. Which was definitely not on the preapproved purchase list from the Bank of Gilliam.

School had become a major source of tension, because I just wanted to hang out on my BBS all the time. I tried to get through my files as quickly as possible so I could go online or sleep. My mom kept complaining to my dad that I was sleeping all day. They finally figured out that it was because I was staying up all night on the computer. Oops. So my parents were not fans of the new modem plan, and my dad was becoming increasingly vocal about his opinion that I was wasting my life. He didn't understand what had captured my attention so thoroughly, and I certainly wasn't going to explain it to him. Leaving out a few details didn't count as lying, did it?

My dad was the enforcer of rules in our household, but it was my mom who made them. Her most important rule was never, ever, to lie—especially not to her. I'd learned this rule early on when, as a six-year-old, I'd discovered that instead of brushing my teeth at night, I could just wet the brush to make it look like I had. But then one night my mom asked me if I'd brushed my teeth, and I lied. I was apparently not quite the clever innovator I thought I was, and I learned that the tooth-brush-wetting trick is on page seventeen in the parents' guide to six-year-olds. After discovering my treachery, my mom sat me down and said: "Jimmy, I know this seems like it doesn't matter, but if I can't trust you on the little stuff, I'll never be able to trust you on the big stuff, when it really does matter." I hadn't lied to my mom since that day. Good people love God and don't lie. So whether or not lying by omission counted as actual lying was kind of a crucial distinction for me. Especially because of Tori.

Andy had introduced me to a number of things that I knew my parents would disapprove of, but it was Tori Amos, a classically trained pianist who had grown up in North Carolina as a preacher's kid, that would have sent my parents to the altar weeping. Tori's songs weren't played on the radio and she was ever so clearly a feminazi. I absolutely loved her music and felt like I was personally betraying Jesus every time I listened to her songs "God," "Crucify," and "Icicle." The internal struggle over whether or not to listen to evil, secular, rock music was a constant source of discussion at my church youth group, but even while agreeing with everyone, I couldn't bring myself to talk about Tori. I was racked with guilt each time I pressed play and heard that the "good book is missing some pages" or "God sometimes you just don't come through." But I didn't stop listening.

Parents Just Don't Understand

I started working at the local grocery store, Harris Teeter, when I was fifteen. I worked as much as the store would let me, determined to earn my own money. My paychecks went to my parents, of course, but I soon figured out how to hack their banking system. To buy things I wanted without them knowing, I needed money that was "off the books." Since I had to eat while on the job, I realized that I could eat cheap food, bring home receipts that weren't mine, and get reimbursed for more than what I'd spent. It was easy to get receipts for a burger and fries from the Chargrill next door, then eat thirty-seven-cents' worth of macaroni and cheese from the frozen-food aisle at the store. With my off-book cash in hand, I biked to the mall and bought cassette tapes and CDs they would never let me buy, like Pearl Jam, Soul Asylum, and Guns N' Roses. Welcome to the jungle, baby!

But the real reason I was so intent on making money was because I needed a lot of it to kick-start my new dream of starting an Internet Service Provider (ISP). Over Christmas, my parents had finally relented and let me buy my new modem. People were connecting faster than ever to Infinity's Edge and I wanted more. I dreamed about having a bunch of computers and giving everyone access to the internet. I created a business plan based around Linux, a new open-source operating system, and I discovered that I could bootstrap it for five thousand dollars. My plan specified that to cut out the cost of an office, I had to run it from home. I told my dad that I needed to install thirty phone lines in the house. He laughed me out of the room. But I was serious!

My mom was becoming increasingly concerned about the possible non-Christian influences of my online world. She wasn't exactly sure that what I was doing on my computer was wrong, but the fact that she could no longer control my inputs bothered her. I had all these "friends" who lived far away and seemed sort of shady to her, and my dad was frustrated that I was continuing to waste my time on a pointless endeavor with no career possibilities. He thought I should be programming, not hanging out with people who went by monikers like "Doppelganger." I was irritated that they were giving me such a hard time. I did all my schoolwork; I wasn't drinking or doing drugs. I was a good kid by any metric.

Of course, I was being increasingly exposed to the non-Christian world. I was working at the grocery store with regular guys, listening to forbidden music, and interacting with many different types of people online. I was hanging out in online subgroups—with punks, Goths, and Tori fans—and learning about people radically different than myself. I made the mistake of standing up for creationism on a Gen-X message board once and got absolutely eviscerated. I was shell-shocked by the tone and derisiveness of the response, but I didn't know what to make of it. In a pre-search-engine era, I was getting information from the people whom I interacted with most frequently online. It was information I'd never had inside my mom's carefully crafted world, and little chinks began showing up in God's armor. My faith in Him was still totally intact, but I was beginning to grow skeptical of certain church teachings. Meanwhile, my mom was plunging ever deeper into the fundamentalist homeschooling community. She started reading Bill Gothard and subscribed to *Gentle Spirit*, a magazine that chronicled the latest advances in homesteading technology alongside earnest arguments about the darkness of lust and the holiness of arranged marriages. It included pullout sewing patterns for colonial-era clothing, which she was thrilled to make but my sisters were less than thrilled to wear.

I worked tirelessly on my dream of starting an ISP and the tension between my parents and me escalated. My dad told me I couldn't get a good job spending all my time online and that if I wanted a future in computers, I should be programming. Taking away my computer became my parents' primary form of punishment. When my dad caught me sneaking out at night to visit the non-Christian girl from the grocery store with the jet-black hair, he locked the computer up for weeks. But I figured out how to unlock it and developed a work-around: I'd pretend to be asleep while secretly listening to my contraband music until my parents went to bed. Then, carefully avoiding the parts of the floor that creaked, I would sneak downstairs, unlock the computer, and stay online all night. I felt guilty about the deception, but the internet was hands down winning the battle for my heart. It was like having a girlfriend that my parents didn't like. They could try to stop me from seeing her, but I was going to sneak out at night. I was in love, and my parents couldn't do anything about it. At least, that's what I thought until I came home from work one day and saw my stash of contraband CDs strewn across my bed.

The music my mom discovered was so far outside the bounds of acceptable Christian listening that my parents didn't know how to react. The sheer volume of Satan's music was almost impossible for them to digest; the cover alone of Soul Asylum's album *Grave Dancers Union* was enough to send me to hell. The records were everything my parents had feared, and they revealed the extent to which I'd been deceiving them in a way that nothing else could have. All my mom wanted was to raise me to be a good, moral person, and this was the proof that something had gone terribly wrong. My mom had failed. She was utterly devastated. My dad, convinced this was the internet's fault, took away my computer completely.

I was adamant that *they* were ruining my life, and they were adamant that *I* was ruining my life. Either way, one thing was certain: my life was ruined. I didn't know what to do, until I found the computer in a hidden storage area in my parents' bathroom. I snuck it out, then put it underneath a pile of dirty clothes in my closet so I could run my BBS without them knowing. Because the computer was supposed to be hidden, my parents initially didn't notice it was gone. I spent a blissful few weeks logging on late at night without interruption. Until, of course, my dad found the computer in my closet and totally freaked. He took the computer and put it on a desk in my parents' bedroom. There was no way I could run my BBS now. They had disconnected me from my entire world, taken away all my friends, and killed my ISP dream, all at once. It was like death to me. So I did the one thing I could think of. I ran away.

I didn't have to spend much time on a rainy park bench to appreciate the realities of the physical world. I had just turned sixteen, and I had no money and nowhere to go. I stayed awake all night in the pouring rain and thought about my predicament. There was no way I was giving up on the ISP. And I absolutely had to run my BBS and be able to get online. But clearly none of that was possible while I was living at home. I had just one option: escape.

RUNAWAY TRAIN

By the time my dad found me in the park the next morning, drenched and shivering, I was ready to play nice. The plan I'd spent all night formulating depended on it.

It was the autumn of 1994, and North Carolina had a law allowing high-school students, even homeschoolers, to enroll in college classes. If I took classes at Wake Tech Community College for two years, got perfect grades, and then applied as a transfer student to the University of North Carolina, I would almost certainly be accepted. And since the classes were so cheap, I would get two years of my college education for only a few hundred dollars. While everyone else was wasting their time in high school, I could enter UNC as a junior. I'd study law, fin-

ish before I was twenty, and go on to specialize in some type of technology law. Or at least
that's what I told my parents. UNC's internet
operation was well known online because the
university ran one of the biggest download sites
and had put the first radio station on the internet. I assumed that as soon as I was at school
and living on my own, I could figure out how
to start an ISP. I just had to get to UNC as
quickly as possible.

The first year of my plan worked perfectly.
Mom believed college was the gateway to a
good life. It was the foundation of doing things
the right way, which would ultimately lead to
meeting a good Christian girl, getting a good
job, having a beautiful family, and being successful in life. Ever committed to my education, she agreed that even though I would be
exposed to various non-Christian elements,
Wake Tech would be better for me than homeschooling. The only problem was that I
couldn't drive. Lessons with my dad had ended
in disaster. Contorting my way-too-tall body
to fit into our Honda hatchback wasn't conducive to operating the clutch properly, and the
frustration drove both of us off the deep end. So
three times a week, my mom drove the forty-

five minutes to Wake Tech, dropped me off, drove home, and then drove back to get me in the late afternoon. It was hard to hate her when she was doing something that awesome for me, so each car ride became a temporary break from the tension at home. I was taking a bunch of political-science and economics classes and bounced my new ideas off her during our daily stops at Hardee's for twenty-five-cent soft-serve ice-cream cones.

My political-science teacher was an ultraconservative Republican consultant killing time between campaigns. I'd been getting the Republican talking points for years, but now I was learning about the underlying theory by reading Friedrich Hayek and Jean-Jacques Rousseau. I started to develop my own relationship to concepts like anarcho-capitalism, glorifying freedom and individual sovereignty. I was so completely certain of my newfound belief in the philosophy of rational self-interest that I even evangelized my mom. I tried to convince her that there was no such thing as altruism, that everything a person does is ultimately about what benefits him. She just raised her eyebrows as I rambled. And ramble I did, oblivious to the irony of saying such things to the woman who spent countless hours patiently driving me back and forth across the state.

I relished my time away from home. I was at an almost-college! I saw things I'd never seen before, like single parents and smoking. People even swore in public and wore Marilyn Manson T-shirts. It was fantastic. Then the online world exploded with buzz about a movie that had just ripped through the Cannes Film Festival. It was hitting the United States on October 14, 1994—my seventeenth birthday. Suddenly my English paper required extra research and I needed to go to UNC's library for the whole day on Saturday the fifteenth. Mom drove me all the way out there, unsuspecting of my secret plan to see Quentin Tarantino's *Pulp Fiction* at the Varsity Theater. I had never seen an R-rated movie on a big screen, let alone one with such graphic violence. I was terrified they would check my ID, but I had my Carolina T-shirt on and easily blended in with all the older students. It probably didn't hurt that I was almost six and a half feet tall. The theater was packed, so I literally had a front-row seat when John Travolta shoved a giant needle into Uma Thurman's chest, and Samuel Jackson quoted Ezekiel before executing one poor motherfucker. The film was disgusting and shocking and utterly non-Christian. I went back to see it again the next weekend.

That same month, the online world changed forever. The World Wide Web was still fairly new and painful to use from home. Mosaic, the first graphical web browser, was optimized for university broadband connections, so if you were using a dial-up modem it would take several minutes to see a web page, and only hard-core people like me were willing to put up with the wait. The public beta release of Netscape changed all that. Netscape was a web browser that let you see the page within a couple seconds; the pictures would fill in while they downloaded. It was the most unbelievable thing I'd ever seen. Netscape had made the internet usable for normals. Now everyone wanted internet accounts, and the number of websites and ISPs exploded. The internet was going mainstream and it was more important than ever that I get to UNC.

I didn't sleep for the next six months. I worked overtime at the grocery store, saving money for my ISP, got straight As at school during the day, and stayed on the internet all night. Year one of my escape plan was almost complete.

Cue parental sabotage.

During the spring quarter, my parents announced that we were moving again—this time to Lynchburg, Virginia, the mecca of Christian fundamentalism. We would attend Jerry Falwell's Thomas Road Baptist Church, where we'd spend our Sundays worshipping on the set of *The Old Time Gospel Hour*. My sisters would go to Falwell's Lynchburg Christian Academy and I would go to his Liberty University. My plans were destroyed.

I was determined not to let my parents ruin my life. I went through every scenario I could think of to preserve my plan. But I wasn't eighteen yet, I couldn't drive, and I had missed the deadline to apply to UNC as a sophomore. The biggest issue was tuition. My parents thought Liberty was exactly what I needed to get back on track, and they refused to pay for any other college. By moving to Virginia, I'd lose in-state tuition for my junior year at UNC, and I wouldn't yet qualify for in-state tuition at any community college in Virginia for my sophomore year. So I had to change their minds.

It was clear to me that we were moving as part of their unending quest to find the community they'd lost upon leaving Los Gatos Christian Church. They'd spent the past seven years trying to find it again, and they had become more and more radical as their search continued. The decision to go to the source, Jerry Falwell, was the ultimate manifestation of their desperation. I told them it was pointless and that they'd just be disenchanted again, as they had been with all the other places we'd tried. My protests didn't matter, of course.

I finished Wake Tech in May, took and passed the GED, and moved to Lynchburg with my family in the late spring. My graduation present was a mission trip to Israel with Dr. Falwell. When we got back, I spent the rest of the summer attending Thomas Road with my parents and refusing to go to Liberty. But in the end, I couldn't bear to waste a year, so a week before classes were scheduled to begin, I succumbed. I told my parents at our Sunday post-church lunch that I would go; I just wouldn't stay in the dorms. They were happy. I was not.

I entered Liberty University as a sophomore in the fall of 1995.

Hot Sex at Liberty University

Going to LU was like being in church all the time. Nowhere was this more apparent than every Monday, Wednesday, and Friday, when Liberty's five thousand students and hundreds of staff members filed into The Vines Convocation Center—Liberty's ten-thousand-seat arena—to attend the mandatory hour-long convocation. Within the first week, I was bored with it and began prepping for my next class during the program. On Friday, a resident assistant motioned to me that I couldn't read during convocation. I was at school, but couldn't read my criminal-justice textbook? I'd been dealing with my parents telling me to do things that didn't make sense for years, and I was sick of it. I stormed out and made a break for the men's bathroom. The RA ran after me and introduced me to the demerit system.

Liberty had a lot of rules, and demerits were your punishment if you broke any of them. Students couldn't hold hands, couldn't be in the other gender's dorms, had to obey the dress code—skirts below the knees for girls, ties for boys—most definitely could not have sex, and absolutely could not have an abortion. That was the worst possible thing. You also couldn't see R-rated movies or, apparently, read during convocation. These things violated the "Liberty Way." What didn't violate the Liberty Way was to meet someone at school and get married. I hadn't understood what people sometimes laughingly called the "MRS Degree," but once I got there, I did. The Vines Center was nicknamed "The Furnace" because it was home to our team, the Liberty Flames, but it was really because the whole school was one big pressure cooker. They threw a bunch of horny teenagers together and let them stew in the cauldron of sexual tension. One excellent way to bring new Christians into the world is to birth them, so the school was designed to marry us as quickly as possible, after which we could make babies and be shipped off to infiltrate every level of society and transform it with our Christian values. Genius! If you can't have sex until you get married, you get married pronto. The whole setup felt fake and manipulative, and I was miserable— trapped in the prison of Liberty.

A few days after my forbidden studying session during convocation, I was desperate to get online and I had heard there was an internet hookup in the library. The room I found wasn't worthy of the word *library*. There were almost no books, and of the few that were there, about half were about Jesus and the rest were crap. They didn't even have a computerized card catalog; it was all still done by hand. But they did, thank God, have two brand-new computers—the only ones on the entire campus connected to the internet. I was the only person using the computers, so I was able to spend all my time there.

During my second week, I was editing my Netscape bookmark file in HTML, which is how the cool kids did it back then, when the deputy librarian came up behind me. He looked over my shoulder at what I was typing, thought it was some kind of sinister computer code, and freaked out. He marched me into the head librarian's office and declared that he'd caught me hacking the computer. The head librarian began interrogating me, saying over and over that the computers were only for accessing the internet. I know, I said, I was just editing my bookmarks! But the two of them were convinced that I was going to take down the school's new computers and leave them with no ability to fix them. I kept trying to explain that I wasn't doing anything wrong and that I wasn't hurting anything, but it didn't matter. They got more and more frenzied and started arguing about what to do with me. I said I could show them what I'd been doing, but they paid no attention. Trying to explain that I wasn't hurting anything to Liberty idiots was the last straw. My contempt for the whole place overwhelmed me and I burst into tears. This finally got their attention, and they started to believe me. While rambling on about how I could no longer do whatever it was I'd been doing, one of them mentioned that there was some guy I should probably meet. Which was how I found Will.

Will was ten years older than me, and he had just been hired to run Liberty's Academic Computing Department. I told him my "hacking" story and we immediately bonded over my traumatic experience. I soon learned that Will's lab was outdated and staffed by computer-science geeks, which was not particularly helpful since no real computer geeks attended Liberty. I told him I wanted to get the entire university on the internet. He asked how often I could come to help. I went every day.

Liberty's lab ran on an older networking technology called Novell. I immediately started exploring how to redo everything in Windows NT, which would allow me to connect the university to the internet. I went from having one personal computer that could connect to other computers over a modem, to having access to a network of computers. I now had the opportunity to create the ISP I had always wanted, while bringing the internet to the entire school and making Liberty safe for everyone who wanted the freedom to edit their bookmarks. I took all the research I had done for my ISP and applied it to this, and in a few months we had replaced all the computers and rebuilt the whole lab.

When we were up and running, the university's administration expressed concern that people would have access to things on the internet that violated the Liberty Way. Will and I told them that there was no way blocking software could really work, and promised to monitor the traffic ourselves. If there were any violations, we said we'd deal with it, making me Liberty's internet cop.

Early one morning a few months later, Will

got a frantic phone call from a physics professor before classes started. He said that every time he typed in a search, it came up "Hot Sex." Will and I were horrified. This was our worst nightmare. We'd been fighting so hard to bring the internet to LU, and this was exactly the kind of thing that could shut us down, especially since it was a professor who had made the discovery. I had to figure out what was going wrong before everyone got on campus. I went to Web-Crawler, the first-ever search engine, typed in a search and, sure enough, got back "Hot Sex." The monitoring software that I'd deployed on our network also happened to be caching software, so when the URL hadn't changed after a few minutes, I realized that the caching software was storing the results of the previous person's search. Someone on campus had searched for "Hot Sex"! And Will and I could find out the exact time of the search and the specific computer that had been used! Who could it have been? Hot on the trail, we scoured through the logs for the original query until we found it. The search had originated from the computer in the math department, the only computer outside the lab or library connected to the internet. At the time of the original search, the person logged on to that computer was none other than the professor who had contacted us about the problem. He'd come in early that morning for a date with "Hot Sex" and then tried another search but "Hot Sex" was clingy. So he went to the computers in the computer lab and, unable to escape from his transgression, completely flipped out. We laughed for about ten minutes straight. Will then apologized profusely to the professor for the system error and told me that if we ever had budget problems this might come in handy. That was the day Will taught me about Machiavelli.

It wasn't long before I started catching and busting other people for looking at porn in the computer lab. It felt wrong to snoop, but I could easily identify porn sites without spying on people by searching for key words like "xxx" in the logs. If I found a violation, I could look up that IP address and see who was logged in to that computer when the site was accessed. What was fascinating to me was that you could only access the internet in public places like the library or lab, so all these guys—I never caught any women—were all looking at porn in public places. Then one day I found something odd. The string of page URLs I'd spotted were definitely pornographic, but not about women. They were about men. With other men. Someone at Liberty was gay! It was the biggest scandal ever! I was about to run into Will's office with the explosive news, but I hesitated. How desperate for an outlet would someone have to be to risk looking at gay porn in the public computer lab—at Jerry Falwell's university?

Dr. Falwell's antihomosexual notoriety was a rallying cry at Liberty. He would give a sermon at convocation and say Christian things, but when he really needed to get the crowd going, he would throw something in about how gays were destroying the United States, and the place would erupt. It was uncomfortable for me. I was a devout Christian, but it didn't seem right that people would get so excited and fired up by hating on gay people. I had interacted with gay people online, especially through Tori's music, and I didn't see anything to hate. I thought about this guy who, like me, probably had been forced to attend Liberty, most likely by his parents. I realized that he must be going through hell—so much so that he was willing to risk everything just to have an outlet for what he was feeling. So I didn't report him.

And I began questioning the antigay zealotry at Liberty.

I also wasn't really feeling Evangelism 101. It was a required class taught by Dr. Danny Lovett. Every class he'd yell, "Jesus is what?" and we had to respond, "Jesus is awesome!" It was really just Sales 101, except the purpose wasn't to teach us to sell electronics or a car, but to teach us how to convert people to Christianity. The way you spread the Word is by telling your story about how you gave your heart to Jesus. For homework, we had to share our testimony with someone, save the person's soul, and then write about how many new soldiers we'd added to God's army. I took it as an opportunity to work on my creative-writing skills.

By my second semester I had figured out how to survive at Liberty. The university's technological backwardness had turned out to be a blessing in disguise. I was responsible for bringing the internet to LU, got to play with a bunch of computers in the lab I had helped create, and I even set up Liberty's first website. And sometimes when the lab was closed, Will and I would get a bunch of people together to play a prerelease test version of Quake, the most graphically violent computer game ever created. We felt mildly guilty as we roamed the catacombs of virtual hell, but we were having too much fun blowing each other up to stop. We were, after all, killing demons. Jesus himself would approve, I'm sure. It still sucked being at Liberty, but at least now I had the internet—and movies. A new movie theater had opened up just a half mile down Liberty Mountain. Movies that had already done their first run showed there for a buck, so breaking one of Liberty's key rules had never been cheaper. I figured that if God didn't want me seeing *Casino*, he wouldn't have made it so convenient. During the day I would go to class or the lab, and later, instead of studying, I'd go to the theater before my dad came to pick me up. I was hacking the Liberty Way.

Toxic Cocktails

In March I began having trouble sleeping at night, and, as a result, my grades were slipping. I couldn't breathe lying down, so I slept in my chair. My mom couldn't sleep either, so we stayed up late together. She made clothes through the night for me and my sisters while I sat upright at my computer. I went to the clinic at Liberty and they told me I had bronchitis. But by spring break, the medicine hadn't done anything. We were installing new computers in the lab at the time, so I didn't want to stop working, but I could barely stand up. I went back to the doctor on campus and he told me I should get an X-ray at Virginia Baptist Hospital in Lynchburg. My dad took me there, and after taking the X-ray, they immediately sent me to Lynchburg General. We were getting worried. My mom had an appointment that day for her insomnia, but she canceled it to be with me at the hospital.

That afternoon they found two liters of fluid around my lungs. Reclining forced the fluid into my lungs, which is why I wasn't able to breathe lying down. They stuck a giant needle in my back and sucked the fluid out. I couldn't stop coughing. But the big concern was why fluid was building up around my lungs in the first place. Late that night I was in the ICU recovering with my parents when the doctor came in and said there was still about half a liter of fluid around my heart. I needed surgery immediately to prevent a heart attack. The heart surgeon and his team were called that night for an early morning surgery, where they would poke a hole next to my heart to drain the fluid. My mom wanted answers. What was going on? The doctor talked around the questions for a while, but then he said the word *tumor*, and I saw the color drain from my parents' faces. After he left, I looked at them, puzzled, and said, "A tumor, is that like, cancer?"

I was eighteen years old. It never occurred to me that I could be *really* sick. Biology and the physical world were not my thing; I didn't really even know what cancer was. But I had seen enough movies to know that if the c-word was invoked, it meant I could die. And my parents knew too. In that moment, our relationship changed forever. All traces of any previous strain or tension evaporated. We were instantly united, with one common goal: keeping me alive.

The next morning I had the heart surgery, which went as well as it could have. The doctors did a biopsy of my lymph nodes to determine if the tumor was malignant, and if it was, whether it was Hodgkin's disease, which was easily treatable, or non-Hodgkin's lymphoma, which was not so easily treatable. Simply put, if I had cancer, did I have the good kind or the bad kind? We were hoping for no cancer at all, but we'd settle for the good kind. The next thing I knew, I was being whisked off to Charlottesville in an ambulance. We were headed to the University of Virginia, which had the best lymphoma and leukemia program in the region. There they figured out that I had a rare form of non-Hodgkin's lymphoma called T-cell lymphoblastic lymphoma, which is the fastest of the fast in terms of fast-growing lymphomas. So, not the good kind.

I wasn't sure how to feel. I knew I was supposed to feel devastated or even depressed. But I didn't. Twenty-four hours earlier I'd been working at the computer lab, and now I was an eighteen-year-old with a really bad case of cancer. The next few hours were a whirlwind of planning. The doctors explained that because my cancer was growing so fast, it should theoretically respond quickly to treatment. There was a 70 percent chance that they could get it, and were hopeful that it was curable.

The treatment they outlined for me was pretty daunting. I was going to receive CHOMP therapy for nine months. It would start right away with a five-week induction phase to be followed by two visits every month, one for five days of methotrexate—the

M in CHOMP—and one for three days of the CHOP cocktail. For the next five weeks I was hammered with chemo. Dr. Falwell, Will, and others from church frequently made the two-hour round-trip from Lynchburg to visit, and I spent the time offline reading my Bible and watching the hospital's private movie channel. I really appreciated the sense of humor of whoever decided to screen *Malice*—in which Alec Baldwin plays a scheming doctor with a God complex—to a hospital full of patients. Well played.

About two weeks into my induction, my mom was sitting by my hospital bed when I noticed how bloated and swollen her feet were. Her face was also kind of puffy, so I reminded her that she was at a hospital with a clinic downstairs and it was all right to leave me alone for a few hours. She went, and was examined by a second-year medical student who, probably as part of an assignment, spent two hours taking her entire medical history. She had been seeing doctors for years about her high blood pressure—which was not responding to treatment and was only getting worse—but no one had ever taken a full history before. So of course this random med student made connections that no one else had and concluded that my mom had Cushing's syndrome. It was great to finally give a name to what had been making her sick, but it merely raised a much bigger question—why did she have it? The doctors did a number of tests and found a tumor on her adrenal gland, which explained why she had been up all night making clothes for everyone instead of sleeping. Now that I knew the t-word led to the c-word, I waited nervously in my hospital room all day for the results of her tests. Late that night, my dad came in and delivered the news.

Mom had cancer too.

We both tried so hard to hold back tears. When he left, I lost it. It was the first time during the whole ordeal that I'd cried.

The little secret about being sick that the healthy don't know is that when it's happening to you, you have something to hold onto: you have the goal of beating it. Everyone is cheering you on, offering support and encouragement. But when it happens to someone else, you have nothing. You have no control, you can't help, and you have very little ability to do anything useful. Being in that situation with my mom made me understand what everyone else was going through with me. It was much, much worse to be a bystander than it was to be sick. How my dad was dealing, I couldn't even imagine. I knew he loved me and it must have been a nightmare to watch me go through this, but my mom . . . my mom was his entire life.

August 25th

Because my cancer was everywhere, the only treatment was chemo. My mom's cancer was in one place, so the surgeons just cut it out. After my induction was over I went back home to Lynchburg. Twice a month my dad would fire up the Gilliam cancer bus and take us to UVA so mom and I could see our oncologist, Dr. Michael Williams, together. In one of those sessions she asked Dr. Williams to look at a bump in her hair. He didn't think it was anything, but she insisted he test it. A few days later, we found out that the cancer had spread through her whole body. The adrenal tumor had been consuming all the resources, and so none of the other cancer cells were able to grow, but when they took the adrenal tumor out, the cancer went everywhere, including her bones. There was nothing they could do; my mom was going to die.

Mother and son both getting rare cancers was a story made for a church of the television age. The congregation of Thomas Road was given updates on us multiple times a week, and the community leaped into action. People brought food and cards and did all they could to help. My sisters were thirteen and fourteen, going to school and just trying to understand what was going on. My dad was the true hero, holding everything together in ways I couldn't even fathom. He was terrified that we would lose our health insurance, so he held down his full-time job, all while driving me to UVA every week, dealing with my sisters, and tending to my mom. He was so busy during the day that most of the time it was just the two cancer patients hanging out at home.

My mom and I bonded during our days together. Dark humor was our favorite coping mechanism. I would call the methotrexate Mountain Dew because of its color; but mostly because calling it urine just wasn't polite. Mom, always focused on my future, suggested I become a cancer doctor because it was clearly a growth industry.

We told each other stories, and I learned stuff about her that I never knew. Like that she was an entrepreneur. She was twelve when she launched her first enterprise. Already a skilled seamstress by then, she made "Merry Xmas" bowties and then enlisted her dad to help her sell them. I told her how I remembered driving all over the place with her searching for fabrics, and she confided that she might have missed her calling by not pursuing sewing. She made me promise never to marry someone who couldn't sew, because she'd waste a ton of money buying clothes. I told her how much I always loved watching her cook, and she confessed how much she hated cooking. She reminded me that when I was really young, I always tried to do things to surprise her, like make her lemonade or brownies all by myself. And when she'd been pregnant during that cold New York winter when my dad was often in Boca Raton, I'd insisted on getting the wood from the outdoor woodpile myself so she wouldn't get hurt.

Mom was on a lot of pain medicine, but she had turned down potentially life-prolonging chemotherapy because she'd witnessed how miserable it was when I went through it. Euthanasia was something we would never consider because we were so pro-life, so this was her compromise: death by omission. She just wanted to spend her last days peacefully looking at the lake behind our house, so Dad set up a bed downstairs in the living room. I tried to take care of her when he was at work, but there was a period when I was having debilitating headaches and had to stay in bed upstairs. I couldn't be upright for more than twenty seconds, so if Mom needed something, I would hobble down the stairs from my bedroom as fast as I could, then lie flat on the ground because I didn't fit on our couch. I'd rest a few minutes, then get what she needed and then go lie down on the ground again. It was ridiculous, but at least we could laugh.

None of us had been to church in months, because we didn't want to leave mom alone, but one Sunday she insisted we go. Of course, it was the Sunday before the Fourth of July—a day more important than even Christmas or Easter at Thomas Road—so everyone was there. Walking through the congregation that day was like walking around with a giant spotlight pinned on my every move. Everyone wanted to know how I was doing, how mom was, how I felt, how my dad was holding up. It was debilitating. All they wanted to do was support me and my family—and all I wanted to do was get away from them.

As Dr. Falwell fired everyone up for the upcoming God and Country rally (the biggest event of the year), I kept wondering how much money was being wasted on it—money that should have been used to buy the books and computers that Liberty desperately needed. The Bible study was irrelevant to me, the Sound of Liberty singers seemed fake, and by the time Dr. Falwell started bashing Clinton and pushing all of us to buy *The Clinton Chronicles*—a documentary "investigating" Clinton's supposed criminal activity and the suspicious deaths surrounding him—I was over the whole thing. I wasn't questioning God, but I was done with the Church. Dr. Falwell never told us to vote for Bob Dole, but when the voter-registration forms were passed down the aisles as the congregation sang "God Bless America," the message was clear. I'd been wanting to vote since I was a kid, but when the forms came to me, I refused to take one.

My dad was upset, and asked me why. I told him I wasn't going to vote because what I did wouldn't make any difference. The church and politics were one and the same to me, so rejecting the church meant rejecting politics. I was no longer a loyal foot soldier in God's army. I went home disillusioned and apathetic, and took refuge in my online world, where no one knew I was sick. Where I was a normal.

And just when it seemed like our situation couldn't possibly get worse, my mom's parents came to help. They were a rare source of tension between my parents because of my grandma's effect on my mom. Appearances were incredibly important to Grandma. She trained schnauzers for dog shows, clipped them to perfection, and proudly paraded them about while calling them her "children." She was the uncontested boss of her family, my grandfather mere furniture. My mom adored and idolized her mother, and she was always trying to please and impress her. None of us knew what to expect from my grandparents' visit this time, but we certainly didn't expect the devastation that followed.

They checked into a nearby hotel, then came to the house. Within only a few minutes of their arrival, Grandma was telling my dad and my sisters what to do. She assured us that she knew what we were feeling and how to properly handle the situation, because she had been through the death of Ricky and Pepper, her two prized schnauzers. In the days that followed, her critiques of how my family was running our household escalated. My dad told her to cut my sisters some slack given the insanity of what they were going through. After attacking my dad for how the girls were being raised and getting nowhere with him, she took her complaints directly to my mom. We'd been trying to buffer her from Grandma's craziness, but now she was smack in the middle of it. My mom resisted, but because she couldn't get out of bed, she was a captive audience for my grandma's repeated assaults. I was outraged that she had to spend what little strength she still had defending herself from the parents that were supposed to be giving her love and support. But my grandmother was determined. She had made it her personal mission to improve her daughter's parenting skills no matter what—an odd focus, given that my mom was dying.

The strain in the house was unbearable. Finally, in an attempt to patch things up, my grandparents offered to do something special for my mom. There was just one thing my mom wanted: a mother-daughter outing with my sister Kristen to get her a locket. She'd already done this with Kelly, and she knew that if she didn't go soon, she'd never get the chance to do it with Kristen. But going out of the house was a huge ordeal. Because the bone cancer was ravaging her body, car rides were dangerous. If her spine moved in the wrong way, she could die. She had to wear a giant brace anytime she left the house. She was really self-conscious about her appearance, but desperately wanted to have this moment with Kristen. My grandparents promised to take them to Lynchburg's only mall.

On the day of the trip, just Kristen, Mom, and I were at home. Kristen spent almost five hours getting Mom cleaned up, doing her makeup, and preparing her to go out in her wheelchair. They were ready and waiting by the door a few minutes before the scheduled pickup time, Mom nervous and excited. Hours passed and it started getting dark. We called the hotel, but we couldn't reach my grandparents. I called my dad and he tried the hotel too. Nothing. That's when we all knew the truth: my grandmother was ashamed of my mom and didn't want to be seen in public with her. Mom had always been the perfect child, my Grandma's trophy. But no longer beautiful, no longer something that would reflect positively back on my grandmother, she was an embarrassment. And she knew it.

I couldn't imagine how my grandparents would try to justify forsaking my mom, but they never said a word about it.

A week later, my dad needed their help. He had to work, but Mom had a radiation treatment scheduled in Charlottesville. So my grandparents agreed to take her in my dad's car, which was the only one that my mom could fit in with her brace. On their way home from the appointment, my grandpa fell asleep at the wheel and totaled the car. Everyone survived, even my mom. She was saved by her brace. My grandpa had minor injuries consistent with someone who had been wearing a seat belt. My grandma had significant injuries consistent with someone who had lied about wearing a seat belt. That night, Mom and I were joking about this latest twist in the disaster movie that was our lives. So after all this, we're going to die in a car crash? We wondered what could possibly happen next. She said, "Jimmy, you should write a book about this someday. No one will ever believe it."

I was lying upstairs in my room a few weeks later when I heard my mom's voice. She wasn't able to talk loudly, so if I could hear her voice all the way upstairs, something had to be wrong. I stumbled out of bed and heard my mom pleading with her parents to leave. She started yelling at them to get out right as I hit the top of the staircase. I looked down and saw my mom—who hadn't moved on her own for three months—frantically trying to crawl up the stairs. Horrified, I rushed down to meet her where she was, and helped her sit up as best I could. Then I told her to stay there.

I don't know what I expected to see when I rounded the corner into the living room, but it wasn't both of my grandparents sitting calmly on the couch. They hadn't moved an inch. Their daughter, so weak she couldn't sit up on her own, had been so desperate to get away from them that she'd crawled off her bed, out of the room, and to the stairs. And they had just sat and watched. They hadn't left like she'd asked; they hadn't helped her or prevented her from hurting herself, they'd just watched. My grandmother's head was ramrod straight, a proud and stern expression on her face as she stared toward the lake. I went ballistic. My grandpa got up and tried to talk to me, so I yelled at him while my grandmother sat stoically beside him. I told them I wouldn't let them hurt her anymore, and that they had better get the hell out right then and there. They did. And then I went back to the stairs to help my mom.

I tried to understand how any of this was possible. I'd spent an awful lot of my time as a Christian talking about Satan and hell, but this was the first time I'd truly seen evil. I saw it up close and personal, and it wasn't some big fiery deity, it was the face of my grandmother staring out at the lake with no compassion or empathy for her daughter.

Mom declined rapidly after that. Dementia set in. One night I heard her talking to herself, and went downstairs to be with her. She was really upset and kept saying, "no one else understands," and, "we're going to beat this; no one else wants us to, but we're going to beat this." The combination of her delusion and paranoia, plus the fact it was true for me but not for her, was more than I could handle. I said,

"Yes, Mom, we're going to beat this." The last thing I said to her that I knew she understood was a lie.

My mom died at 4:46 p.m. on August 25, 1996. I watched Dr. Falwell bury her three days later. By Thanksgiving, my treatments were over. I was nineteen and cancer-free.

ESCAPE FROM THE EVANGELICAL GHETTO

I knew after my mom died that there was no point in wasting the life I'd been given trying to do things the right way. My mom had done everything she was supposed to do. She did well in school. She went to a prestigious college. She got married, had kids, and spent her days teaching her children, sewing her family clothes, and being a supportive wife. She was an exceptionally good person who had even moved her whole family closer to the church she believed in. She'd been one of God's best soldiers. And in the end it hadn't mattered. He'd killed her anyway, and forced my dad to watch as the life was slowly ripped out of the person he loved most.

I didn't know why God had taken her and not me. Why did I deserve to live but she hadn't? I owed it to my mom to make my life matter and to succeed like she'd always wanted me to. I just couldn't do it her way. Life was short, and mine just might be very short. I decided that the "right way" was wrong. So I did the one thing she wouldn't have wanted me to do. I quit college and set out to prove to the world—and to her—that this decision wouldn't ruin my life.

Live Free or Die

I knew that the internet was my ticket out. Companies like Netscape were popping up everywhere, and, all of a sudden, the internet seemed like it could provide a real career path. So I went back to work in the computer lab with Will, and I began plotting how to get out of Virginia. I was known as the Internet Kid within Lynchburg's tiny tech community and by all three IT people who were building corporate computer networks in the area. One of them, Brad Warner, was a devout Christian.

He traveled around helping businesses with their computers, and if he had questions about the internet, he'd come to me. A week or two after I returned to the lab, he started consulting with a start-up in the Boston area called Archive Technologies. The company was going to compile a large archive of technical information and sell it online for a subscription fee. In one of his meetings with the founders he told them, "If you want to put all this on the internet, you need to talk to this kid from Lynchburg."

My meeting with the founders went very well. A combination of relatively poor social skills and no fear meant that I just said everything straight. They'd tell me what they were doing, and I'd say, no that's all wrong, you need to do it this way. The fact that I was saying all this to Fred Wang, the former president of Wang Labs, whose dad had founded Wang Computers and invented the word processor, never occurred to me. I just called it like I saw it. At the end of the meeting they said they wanted to hire me and move me to New England. They asked for my salary requirements, and I randomly threw out eighty thousand dollars a year. They said, how about seventy-five?

I accepted, went home, and asked Will to teach me how to drive.

The company was located on the border of New Hampshire and Massachusetts, and they found me a painstakingly refurbished duplex in Hampton, New Hampshire. I bought a used 1988 Acura Legend with the money I had saved up for the ISP and moved in. It was January 1997. Around the same time, my dad decided to move with my sisters to Plano, Texas, just outside of Dallas. He'd flirted briefly with the idea of becoming Liberty's first chief technology officer, but he too wanted a fresh start in a new place. So my remaining family was now almost two thousand miles away from me. I tried to keep going to church, but there were no evangelical churches—let alone megachurches—in New England, so for the first time in my entire life, I had Sunday mornings free. Things couldn't have been more different than they had been only a few short months before. No mom, no family, and no church. I was on my own.

I worked constantly, teaching myself new technologies, gaining confidence in my abilities. It was nearly a month before I realized that I could do whatever I wanted, even in the physical world! I was free, for real. New Hampshire had some great record stores and I became a regular at Newbury Comics. Five or six CDs a week didn't even put a dent in my fat new paycheck. I bought Tori bootlegs and became the guy who impressed the hipster record-store girl with my obscure import purchases. I started going to the movies a lot until one night, it hit me—I could go to concerts. I'd never been to a real rock concert before, and when I looked online, I saw that the Smashing Pumpkins were playing in Amherst—only three hours away!—that week.

Chemo sucks for many reasons, but the most obvious one is that it causes you to lose your hair. It is one thing to be eighteen and 6'9". It is quite another to be eighteen, 6'9", and totally bald. I really couldn't have been more conspicuous—or looked more like a skinhead. At one of the spontaneous potlucks that happened at our home while I was sick, one of my sister's friends said I looked like Billy Corgan. Obviously I hadn't been watching much MTV, but the video for "1979" had just come out, and suddenly it didn't feel like such a bad thing to be bald. Billy had single-handedly turned something traumatic into something almost cool. I had to lose my concert virginity to the Pumpkins. The day of the show I left work early, made the drive to Amherst, got my ticket from will-call, and tried to look like I'd done this before. The music started and everyone leaped out of their seats. So I stood up, too. And when Mr. Corgan promised to "crucify the insincere," my body started to sway in an almost rhythmic fashion. That too was a first. Fundamentalists don't dance.

Dancing was almost as much fun as my new job—designing a system to organize a huge archive of technical product information and putting it online. I figured out that the way to do it was to tag the products with what I called "properties," not to put them in hierarchical categories like Yahoo did. The founders of the company, Fred Wang and Jeffrey Stahl, saw the beauty of this concept right away. They invited me to have dinner in Boston at Jeffrey's penthouse apartment. His place overlooked the harbor and I was more than a little bit nervous because I didn't know why I was there and I'd never been to a fancy dinner at a rich person's house before. As it turned out, they just wanted to tell me that they knew their original plan was outdated and that the only way to go forward was to do it all on the internet. And they were going to pivot the company to pursue my way of organizing information. They wanted to ditch their other partner and replace him with me so I could execute the idea as the new CTO. They offered me 5 percent of the company. I said 10. It was on.

Though my new life was going great, I couldn't quite put the past behind me. I was feeling weak and knew I should see a doctor. During one of our joint visits to see Dr. Williams when it seemed like my mom and I were both well on our way to recovery, we had asked what was next for us. The doctor told me that there was a 50 percent chance I would get cancer again in the first few years after my treatment, and that if this happened, I would most likely die. But if I made it three years, I was pretty much home free. As it had been only five months since the end of my treatment, I was worried that something was wrong.

My new doctor, Dr. David Fisher, was at the Dana-Farber Cancer Institute, which was affiliated with Harvard University and was the largest comprehensive cancer center in the world. He taught at Harvard Medical School and did tons of research, so like many doctors, he saw patients only at "clinic"—which took place only one or two days a week. I'd never been to a clinic before and was unprepared for what it was like. The waiting room was full of people in varying stages of sickness: some with no hair, some with IVs in their arms, others in wheelchairs or with intense scars. I'd never been around so much cancer in such a small space before. I went in for a few tests administered by nurses, then sat in the waiting room terrified. My hands wouldn't stop shaking, and I kept thinking there was no way I'd be able to tell my dad if I had cancer again. Dr. Fisher came out with my test results and said not to worry, that everything was fine. Relief swept over me. I got out of there as quickly as I could, went home and told myself that I really was done with cancer. I had my new awesome life, and to symbolize moving on, I took out the bag with all the cards people had given me, dumped them in a trash can, and burned them.

Soon after, the company moved to Jeffrey's office in Boston. I commuted into the city by bus until I found a loft in an old piano factory in the South End. I moved into it in June. We changed the company's name to the Athink Group and got to work raising ten million dollars. My favorite thing about living in the city was that I didn't need a car. I could even walk to work. But as the weeks went by, walking became harder and harder, and I was getting weaker. So I set up another appointment with Dr. Fisher, assuming that I just had a bad case of the flu.

The waiting room at the clinic was completely packed on the day of my appointment, and I had to wait for hours to see the doctor. But unlike at my last visit, I wasn't nervous at all. I was sure things were fine and that I was just overreacting. I read every issue of *Entertainment Weekly* to keep myself occupied until, finally, Dr. Fisher called me into his office. I've never forgotten the look he had on his face when he said my name. I followed him down the hallway, and when I sat down he told me that I had leukemia.

It was the same cancer as before, he said, but it had spread into my blood. All I could think was: I'm dead; it's over. It took me a while to start talking, but I finally said that my understanding from my last doctor was that if the cancer came back, nothing could be done. He assured me that there was something we could try. It was a long shot, he explained, but

I could get a bone-marrow transplant if we found a donor. Siblings were the most likely to be a match, but we already knew that my sisters weren't. Dana-Farber would go to the national bone-marrow registry to search for an anonymous donor. The chances of finding a match were about 10 percent, maybe slightly better because I was of Irish descent. If I'd been black or Asian there would have been almost no hope, which put a whole new spin on the concept of white privilege. If they found a donor and did the transplant, there was a 30 percent chance that it would work. And 30 percent was better than dead. I kept thinking about how I was going to tell everyone at work so I didn't have to think about how I was going to tell my dad. I asked how long I had before I needed to check in to the hospital. Dr. Fisher said I had a week.

I took the subway home in a daze. When I got to my place, there was a message on my answering machine from Dr. Fisher saying it couldn't wait; I needed to come in the next morning. I looked at the phone with dread in the pit of my stomach, then picked it up, and called my dad to tell him the one thing he had prayed never to hear again. I went to work the next morning and told everyone at the start-up that had just reorganized around my idea that I had cancer. I checked into the hospital an hour later.

Before a patient gets a bone-marrow transplant, the doctors have to kill off as much of the cancer in your body as they can. And you need to stay alive while a donor is found. So when I checked in that morning, I was walking into another induction. But unlike my first induction, I was going to have several different kinds of radiation in addition to chemo. And they had to do some targeted radiation on my chest because that's where the cancer had originated. There, and in my balls.

I was told that the reason the cancer had come back was because it had hung out in what they call a "sanctuary site" before spreading to my blood. In this case, the sanctuary site was my left testicle. I was a bit of a prude to begin with, but became even more uptight after my mom died, because I couldn't shake the idea that she could see me from heaven. So I wasn't really paying much attention to what was going on in that region of my body, or it might have occurred to me to mention to Dr. Fisher that one of my balls was supersized. Whoops.

That's one lesson they don't teach you in Sunday school: Masturbate or Die.

After being neglected for so long, my testicles were about to see a lot of action. My Christian upbringing definitely did not make me more comfortable with this, and I struggled against overwhelming embarrassment as I was jostled and arranged by numerous technicians. To make sure the radiation got to the right place, and because they couldn't risk the ink moving even slightly on my body, they permanently tattooed me with little dots. It was unglamorous and felt like a violation, mainly because I was being treated like a slab of beef. It didn't help that the room was, freezing, just like a meat locker. There's no room for feelings when someone is coldly and professionally doing their job—even if that job is tattooing your crotch.

It seemed like Operation Nuke Jim's Balls was being carried out by a parade of rejects from Bedside Manners 101. As we were getting set up on the first day, a technician nonchalantly mentioned that I wouldn't be able to have kids anymore. The next day a doctor I hadn't seen before threw out the possibility that they'd have to "cut it off." No one had even let on that this was a possibility and I was terrified. When I next saw Dr. Fisher I was embarrassed, but I gathered the courage to ask him if it was true. He felt terrible and assured me that no, that was not going to happen. I never saw that other doctor again, and can only imagine the schooling he got. "You told a nineteen-year-old kid that we were going to cut off his testicle?" Definitely not a good plan.

My dad and sisters flew out to be with me during that first week, but didn't stay very long. There was major drama in the new Texan household, and the relationship between my dad and sisters had become tense. Within the first day of their visit they were fighting, so I told them all to just go home. My family was completely disintegrating and I couldn't deal. The people from work were my only friends, and they became my support system, despite the fact that they'd known me for only six months. Fred and Jeffrey both had personal experience with cancer—Fred's daughter and Jeffrey himself had had it—so both were incredibly understanding. All my colleagues, in particular Madeline Mooney, the company's marketing VP, got me through. They brought me a CD player and a bunch of my favorite

CDs, and they visited me all the time. My bedside guests were much different from the year before. There was an atheist, a nonpracticing Catholic, and no one who identified as Christian, as far as I could tell. It took some doing, but we finally set up the internet so I could work and, though the connection kept getting interrupted, I lost myself as best as I could online. I read Web pages this time, not my Bible.

I was a week away from being done with induction 2.0 when all hell broke loose. Because chemo is so toxic, the doctors had to constantly monitor my blood levels to see how far they could push me with the treatments. Below a certain level, the immune system is jacked and there are certain things you can't eat. This was true for almost everyone on the cancer floor, and we all had signs on our doors with our food restrictions. Completely unknown to me, mine said no raw food. How someone ever mistakenly gave me fresh fruit is still a mystery, but someone did. Soon after, a nurse discovered blood in my stool and called the doctor. It was a weekend, so Dr. Fisher and my other regular doctors weren't around, and the on-call doctor she spoke to said not to worry about it.

But the nurse was worried. So she went over the doctor's head and started making noise. She made a lot of people mad, at significant risk to her career, but she fought for me.

I was shitting so much blood that the nurse decided to take me to the ICU herself, where I was immediately placed in critical condition. It turned out that the fruit had caused a major infection in my bowel that was spiraling out of control. If she hadn't gotten me there when she did, it would have been too late to get me the blood I needed. I was losing so much blood so quickly that they infused me with two different bags of blood at the same time. This is dangerous and they rarely do it because it eliminates the doctor's ability to monitor and control a patient's reaction to each individual bag of blood, which come from different donors. But it worked and I stabilized. The trouble-making nurse had saved my life.

Then came the many grueling weeks of recovery. I ate through a feeding tube, lost even more weight, and was in intense pain almost constantly. I was forced to lose any remaining shyness about my body as I gave in to the fact that every nurse in the building would at some point be wiping my ass or adjusting my genitals.

They originally put me on a morphine drip, but it made me nauseated, so they changed it to Dilaudid, which I knew from the film *Drugstore Cowboy* as pharmaceutical-grade heroin. My brain was the only part of my body that was still working, so jacking it up on drugs was the last thing I wanted. They gave me a button to push. If I pressed it, the pain would go away, but I'd lose the one thing that made me me. I tried so hard not to push it. But, in the end, I gave in—over and over and over again. Every time I pressed it, I felt defeated and broken. I just wanted it to end. God had forsaken me.

But the doctors hadn't. It took a while, but they slowly weaned me off the Dilaudid, and I eventually started physical therapy. When I walked a few steps for the first time everyone around cheered, and not just because I was so tall that the hospital gown didn't cover much. I towered over them all, a skeletal giant in a miniskirt. By the time I was stable enough to leave, an extra month had passed.

At home I waited, wondering if they would find a donor while trying not to puke up the disgusting protein shakes I was supposed to drink. It was critical that I eat a lot of calories, because the immediate threat to my life was not cancer; it was losing weight. I had physical therapy every day, and struggled to walk up even one step of the stairs—I'd gone from athletic to barely functioning in eighteen months. I knew there were no guarantees that they'd find a donor, so during the many months of waiting, I worked all the time, trying to do as much as possible while I could.

In August, the doctors told me they'd finally found a match. The transplant was scheduled for September, and in the weeks leading up to it, I kept wondering about the donor. How had he felt when he picked up his phone and someone on the other end said he was the one person on the planet who could save a stranger's life?

When it was finally time, I checked in to the hospital to kick off the sequel to Operation Nuke Jim's Balls. This time they weren't just trying to kill off my cancer cells, they were also trying to kill off my bone marrow. So in addition to the targeted radiation, I lay in an oven for twenty minutes a day for full-body radiation. They also did intensive chemo and TLI—total lymphoid irradiation—in an attempt to kill every last bit of cancer before the transplant. It wasn't fun, although I did enjoy telling the nurses I was going off to get baked. What I didn't know was that my doctors were in heavy deliberations about a critical part of my transplant.

A new technique had recently surfaced in the medical community. By removing the T cells from a donor's marrow before giving it to the patient, it was possible for patients to live out the rest of their lives without taking any immune suppressants or antirejection medications. In my case that would be a huge win, because my risk of getting cancer again would be very high with a suppressed immune system. But the procedure was experimental and risky. So the doctors deliberated and, just a few days before my transplant, Dr. Fisher decided that the possibility of me surviving the transplant and living a normal life without immune suppressants outweighed the risks.

The day of the transplant was tightly scheduled. The donor went into the hospital at some faraway location and had a giant needle stuck in his hip. The doctors extracted a tiny bit of marrow. I had the same procedure done to me in case the transplant failed and they had to reinject me with my own marrow. The extraction is extraordinarily painful, and I wondered why my donor had gotten registered in the first place. Like the nurse, he had gone out of his way, at great personal discomfort and inconvenience, to help a stranger. I added another unknown person to the list of people who'd saved my life.

After the marrow was flown in, the doctors hooked it up to my rack of IVs. It looked like any other bag of blood, only smaller. Groggy from all the Benadryl, I watched as the marrow emptied into my arm. That was the transplant. It couldn't have been more anticlimactic. Fourteen days later I walked out of the hospital alone, my body replenished with the blood of a stranger. It was the fastest recovery from a bone-marrow transplant anyone had ever seen. Doing it T-cell depleted had worked, the whole transplant was a major success, and the clinic staff marveled every time I came in for checkups.

The first day after a long hospital stay is like seeing the world for the first time. I'd always been in a car with my dad driving me home, but this time I took a cab. I looked out the window at the city, and everything looked so real. I knew I was supposed to be worried about graft versus host rejection, but I was a two-time welterweight cancer-fighting champion. There was just one thing on my mind during that bumpy cab ride home: I wonder if DSL is available at my apartment yet?

Yahoo Killer

Athink's funding fell through while I was sick, so we began shutting the company down. I was the last to go, finally leaving at the beginning of 1998. Madeline took a job as the VP of marketing at Lycos and told the CEO, Bob Davis, that he should hire me. The night before my interview with Lycos's VP of development, Dave Andre, and its VP of engineering, Sangam Pant, I scoured their website. And found bugs. So when they took me out to lunch the next day, I ripped apart one of the most successful websites in the world. Dave stepped away from the table, made a call to alert someone about the bugs, and then offered me a job. They didn't actually have a position open, but they wanted to create a new team to integrate all their products. With me on board, they officially created the "integration team," of which I would be half. My boss, Dennis Doughty, and I were given free rein to see what we could pull off.

It was exhilarating to be back in the game again, a twenty-year-old college dropout with stock options, working at the center of the internet revolution. But I was overwhelmed. I'd only ever worked on a team with a half-dozen people, and Lycos was a huge company with hundreds of employees. All the developers seemed much smarter and more experienced than I was, and I was struggling to understand all the different proprietary technologies Lycos had created. As I dug in, I realized that the scope of the problems was immense. I was paralyzed. I didn't know where to start. At the end of my first week I passed Dave Andre's office on my way out for the night. No one else was around and he waved me in. He asked how everything was going, so I was honest and told him what I was feeling. With no hesitation, he dropped the most influential piece of advice I've ever received. He said, "Jim, you can code. You have all the power. Just go do it." So I did.

Lycos was a search engine, and like all search engines at the time, it was trying to figure out how to make money. The key was to make our search engine into something that would appeal to advertisers. Like Excite and Yahoo, Lycos paid the browser, Netscape, to send traffic our way, and we were all trying to keep people on our sites longer, because the longer people were on our sites, the more ads they saw. Lycos's CEO, Bob Davis, was a sales guy, and his strategy was to cut deals with new, venture-funded dot-coms and split the revenue on all the ads that we sold. We would increase our ad inventory, help the start-ups, and the Lycos logo would be all over the web.

I didn't really care about all that. I cared about our search results, which seemed to be the one thing that no one was paying attention to. We were a search engine, but our results sucked, mainly because it took between six and nine months to refresh the search catalog. This meant that even our partner sites didn't show up in our search results, making the entire sales strategy pointless. If I could fix this, our search would be better and we'd actually sell more ads.

So I created an internal web-based tool called LINK to manage all the information from our partner sites and publish out a new, much smaller, search database every day that could be merged into the main search results. If someone searched for Los Angeles weather, we would show a picture with the current weather for L.A. If the user clicked it, he'd be routed to Lycos Weather, powered by one of our partners. If she searched for Boston Red Sox, we would show her the previous night's box scores. The people cutting the partner deals were thrilled. Dennis, LINK, and I were heroes, and our little team was promoted to be in charge of Lycos's most important page: search. It was now officially our responsibility to make sure that we were pushing out the best search results on the internet. Which meant that we had to take on Yahoo.

Yahoo was unquestionably the most popular site on the internet, due to its huge directory of websites curated by several hundred full-time editors. So, for roughly forty million dollars, Lycos purchased a company called WiseWire, which trained machines to categorize webpages. It was the key element in Lycos's plan to beat Yahoo. There was just one small problem: WiseWire sucked. A few months later, Netscape quietly acquired a small company called NewHoo, which intended to compete with Yahoo by having volunteers curate the links instead of paid staffers. It was genius. Getting paid to categorize websites all day gets boring fast, but when you're doing it in your free time on a topic that you know a lot about, it's fun. Netscape had outflanked everyone. Yahoo was using paid editors, Lycos was using machines, and Netscape was using volunteers. I knew immediately Netscape was going to win.

Then Netscape upped the ante by open-sourcing NewHoo and renaming it the Open Directory Project (ODP). A fundamentally open project with volunteers loosely coordinated around a technology platform was a revolutionary new model for getting things done on the internet. This could completely undercut Yahoo if enough volunteers signed up. But Netscape couldn't really do much to promote it because they made millions of dollars from redirecting searches from the Netscape browser to search engines like Lycos. They would be pillaging their own revenue stream. But I realized that if Lycos adopted the ODP, people would flock to volunteer, because their work would be seen by millions, which, in turn, would feed the Lycos search engine. If Lycos relied on the internet and volunteers and chose to put their full weight behind the ODP, it would become the biggest thing out there. A directory that was broad, authoritative, and free? Yahoo would never be able to hire people fast enough to compete. And that's how we'd beat them.

The idea caught on internally—earning me the moniker Yahoo Killer—but it was highly controversial because it meant we didn't need the company we'd just paid millions for. The WiseWire folks argued against the idea because Lycos wouldn't own the ODP. But Lycos had just acquired another company, Wired Digital, and when they got wind of my plan, they wanted their search engine, Hotbot, to use it, too. A few months later, in April 1999, Lycos stopped using WiseWire, and flipped both Lycos and Hotbot—two of the biggest search engines on the internet—to the Open Directory Project. The press was stunned. Even Netscape was surprised. The ODP, invented by Chris Tolles and Rich Skrenta, was given rightful attention for being what it was, a revolutionary industry first. Lycos's participation took it to the next level and the ODP started to explode. As predicted, there was a huge incentive for people to participate because, through our distribution channels, there was a massive audience for their work. With over one hundred thousand categories, ODP quickly dwarfed the Yahoo directory. All the information fed into LINK, which we supplemented with sites in our ad network, before pushing everything back into our search results. Having your listing on the ODP meant power and visibility. It became the most authoritative directory on the internet, and it ultimately grew to over four million sites organized by eighty thousand editors all over the world.

I received a really big award at Lycos's all-company retreat that summer.

A few months later, our team made a huge discovery. In our ongoing efforts to make search results better, Dennis set up an eye-tracking lab and began scientific testing of how people used search. We watched where people looked on the pages and noticed something shocking: people didn't look at the ads. Not only that, but the more we tried to make the ads stand out, the less people looked at them. Our entire advertising philosophy was based on making ads flashy so people would notice them. But we saw, quite counterintuitively, that people instinctively knew that the good stuff was on the boring part of the page, and that they ignored the parts of the page that we—and the advertisers—wanted them to click on.

This discovery would give us an edge over everyone in the industry. All we had to do was make the ads look less like ads and more like text. But that was not what the ad people wanted, and the ad people ran Lycos. The advertiser was seen as our true customer, since advertising was where our revenue came from. Our team argued that our customers were also the people searching, and without them, we'd lose the advertisers. The eye-tracking revelation wasn't enough to convince them, so we tried another tack.

In the ultracompetitive world of search engines, the biggest factor aside from the quality of the results was how fast they loaded. We were constantly trying to take things out of the pages to make them load faster. So I created a program that took queries coming into our site and ran them on all the major search engines, ranking them in order of speed. Yahoo was the fastest and Lycos was down near the bottom. In order to get the company's attention, Dennis set up a computer in a main hallway to show the results in real time. We started pushing to make the pages lighter, and specifically, to make the ads text—or at least make the images in the ads much smaller. We pushed and pushed but the executives kept pushing back, telling us that that was not how the advertisers wanted it. We knew that what the advertisers wanted was bad for them and for us, but no one would listen.

Part of the problem was the treadmill of quarterly earnings reports. Lycos was the fastest company to ever go public. We were a publicly traded company in which all the employees had stock options, so the mood of the company rose and fell along with the stock price. Every quarter you tell shareholders how much profit you made. If it's less than they think you should have made, the stock price goes down, employee morale goes in the toilet, some employees leave for other companies, and the company descends into a death spiral. So we had to hit not our own quarterly revenue targets, but the press's quarterly revenue targets—no matter what. Ideas that could help the company in the long term but that might have a negative impact on quarterly earnings were shot down. Which meant that we had millions of people coming to our website every day and telling us what they wanted, but we were giving them something else. It was only a matter of time before the treadmill killed us.

Then a new search engine came on the scene that was getting a lot of buzz. Less than a year later, Google released its ad product—and it was all text. They had seen the same thing our team had seen in the eye-tracking lab, and because Google was data and engineering driven, they made the right decision. While we were focused on giving advertisers what they wanted, Google told advertisers what they needed. Google knew that people would be more likely to click on ads relevant to their original search queries. If someone searches for "Red Sox" they might click on ads for tickets or scores, but they won't click on a beer ad, no matter how flashy it is, because it's not what they want right at that moment. This was the exact opposite of what the advertising world thought, because they were still operating with a television mindset. But Google was willing to trade the short term for the long term, and they owned the industry as a result. They had figured out how to align the interests of the user and the advertiser. Advertisers weren't allowed to buy ads that weren't useful on searches, which was great for users, and advertisers no longer had to pay for ads no one was clicking on. When Google launched its ad program, it was the beginning of the end for Lycos.

Everyone kept framing my fight to give users what they wanted as a matter of purity, which baffled me. There were people who didn't think you should make money on the internet, but I wasn't one of them. I just thought you should make money on the internet by creating something useful that people wanted. It was obviously the only long-term way to be successful when alternatives were only a click away. The entire industry was being driven into a ditch by idiot MBA hucksters who saw the internet as a resource to plunder for gold. They had no respect for the most beautiful thing ever created, and I hated that Lycos was more than happy to sell them ads. Our entire business was being propped up by the money changers in the temple. I was disgusted. I wanted to make something great that I could be proud of, not swim in a cesspool with the bottom-feeders.

One day, Shumeet, Lycos's chief scientist, ran to my desk and said I had to see something. We went to his office where he showed me a new program that allowed him to see and download music that was on other peoples' computers. Whoa! I asked him what the program was called and he said, "Something weird, like Napster?" I'd never really hung out with him before and was pleasantly surprised by the visit. I didn't realize that I was being wooed.

A few weeks later, Sangam, our VP of engineering, told me that he and Shumeet were leaving Lycos to join eCompanies—a Los Angeles–based company created by Jake Winebaum, who ran Disney's online operation, and Sky Dayton, the founder of Earthlink, a hugely successful ISP. eCompanies was going to be an incubator of other internet companies. The premise was that it wasn't the idea behind a business that mattered, but how quickly and effectively that idea was executed. Shumeet had apparently convinced Sangam that they needed someone who could actually build things, so Sangam offered me the position of chief architect. My role would be to advise the tech teams of each new company on how to best build its products. Go start a bunch of internet companies in California? Um. Yes, please. It was my dream job. I knew leaving Lycos was risky because I had a boatload of stock options, and if I waited for them to fully vest, they could be worth several million dollars. Going would mean leaving all that on the table. But Lycos clearly didn't get it, and eCompanies was where I wanted to be. So I left at the end of 1999. I was so adamant about being completely done with Lycos that I sold all my shares immediately, instead of obsessing over when to cash out.

When I sold ended up being at the height of the market. All the stock options I'd left on the table were worth almost nothing a year later.

The Red-Eye

I headed west right after New Year's, and I started working for eCompanies on January 17, 2000. I had a new job on a new coast in a new millennium. I acclimated to Los Angeles quickly, mainly because I never saw any of it. I was consumed with work. In the mornings I would drive down Barrington in Brentwood to Coffee Bean and get a red-eye—a brewed coffee with two shots of espresso. At work I ate Starburst licorice and drank Mountain Dew and coffee. Sangam, Shumeet, and I became such an effective and tight team that the two of them made me an honorary member of the

Indian mafia. It was the best compliment ever.

The flagship company being incubated at eCompanies was Business.com. Business.com was supposed to be the Yahoo of business, and it was Jake Winebaum's primary focus. They had even spent $7.5 million—a record figure at the time—to get the domain name. The company had big plans for the site and had contracted with USInteractive, a Web-outsourcing company, to build it. After five months, with millions of dollars spent, and over thirty people working on the site, they hadn't published a single webpage. eCompanies was all about execution; if our flagship company couldn't launch on time, we were done. So Jake came to me and asked if I could save it. He said that all they really needed was a search engine and a directory. And it had to be live in exactly seventeen days. Could I do it? There was no way I could say no to a challenge like that.

The first thing I had to do was get to the development team. Because there were so many people working on the site, they were in a separate office in Brentwood. What I found there was not good. Calling it an office was too nice. It was more like a sweatshop. Thirty developers were crammed together with all their computers emitting heat in a room where the air-conditioning hadn't worked for weeks. It was summertime in California and it was hot. The conditions were miserable, and the developers were not talking to one another. The situation was not salvageable. I went back to Jake and told him that I wanted to fire the entire USInteractive team. I would keep a couple of core people and bring them back to the Santa Monica office, where we'd make it happen. Jim McGovern, the president of Business.com, thought I was completely nuts and said no way. But Jake overrode him and let me do it. That first night I wrote the code to publish webpages for the entire directory. Now I just needed to make the search engine.

The next seventeen days were batshit crazy. What USInteractive had built wasn't working, because it was way too complicated. So I created a simpler, entirely new architecture for the site. But because the USInteractive system was so complex, it had required dozens of computers and a giant database machine. Since they'd already blown the hardware budget, I had to use those machines, which meant they had to be reconfigured to accept my new architecture, something akin to creating a race car out of a broken 747. Since I was the only one who knew the architecture, I had to do it all myself. And because it was a complete overhaul, I couldn't connect to the computers from the office. I had to actually go to where they were.

All the machines had been set up at Exodus—a secure, earthquake-proof hosting facility near Los Angeles International Airport. Hundreds of dot-com companies had their servers there, so you had to be preapproved and fingerprinted before getting in. Hosting facilities are designed to be computer friendly, not human friendly, so just like the hospital, it was freezing cold and miserable, and all I wanted to do was leave. I think that's why the place was called Exodus. Every night I worked in a cage somewhere in El Segundo, then drove back to the office in Santa Monica to code. But it was worth it.

On the morning of the seventeenth day, I was interviewed by CNN. I had barely slept in two and a half weeks, but I was the happiest person in the world. We had done it. That afternoon, Jake asked me to be Business.com's CTO. I was a controversial choice because of my age, but they didn't really have any other options; I was the only one who knew how anything worked.

That night, I collapsed into bed. I was twenty-two years old and one of the youngest CTOs in history. I was in charge of forty people, and I was making a ton of cash doing what I loved. Without a college degree. Without having done things the "right way." The world had officially been proven wrong. My life was not ruined. It was awesome.

PEACE

The bag was heavy and awkward. I shifted my weight and kept dragging it, looking back nervously at the giant pine trees dancing across the darkened lawn. Terror coursed through me. Was I being watched? I had to hurry. In the door, up the stairs. In my bedroom, I stopped, letting the heavy load lie on the floor. It would just be until I figured out what had happened and what to do, I reminded myself. I looked at my mother's motionless body for another minute and then rolled her under my bed. A siren started wailing.

I jerked awake, disoriented, and I clawed for the ringing phone. The clock read 6:54 a.m.

"Yeah?"

"Jim, are we going in to the office today?"

"What? Why? Is the site down?"

"Turn on your television."

I made my way to the TV, trying to shake off the recurring nightmare that had haunted me for the past year. I reached for the remote and stared as the second tower of the World Trade Center fell.

Think Different

I was thirteen when I first discovered the gothic subculture online. I didn't know anything about the goths except that they looked about as un-Christian as humanly possible, with, perhaps, the exception of actual Satanists. But I couldn't resist checking out their music and, after falling in love with Sisters of Mercy and Siouxsie and the Banshees, I became drawn to the culture's romantic, religious imagery and its comfort with death and darkness. Where else was it not a bad thing to be deathly pale, tall, and skinny? I dreamed of one day visiting Manhattan's legendary goth club The Batcave. But in all my years of working, I'd never taken any time off. Some major product launch always happened in the fall, so my summers were spent cramming, and every August I would politely decline yet another invitation to Burning

Man. Then, in May 2001, I learned that Björk was playing Radio City Music Hall later in the year, and decided that that was the perfect time to take my first break. Which is how I ended up in New York City three weeks after 9/11.

The city I set foot in that September in no way resembled the New York I remembered. Penn Station was overflowing with memorials; the huge walls of flags and flowers seemed never ending. The usual buzz of the city was gone, replaced by a heavy quiet. Missing-person photographs posted by desperate loved ones were everywhere; the station protected at gunpoint by military guards. I found myself unconsciously walking toward Ground Zero, joining others who were silently circling the perimeter. The air was thick with soot and the only sound was coughing. Shop windows were covered in debris and makeshift memorials lined the streets. I made my way through Wall Street, where military personnel stood beneath the famous sign. And then I arrived at Battery Park and saw something that I'd never seen in a U.S. city—tanks. Battery Park was filled with tanks. New York City was a war zone.

My graduation trip to Israel in the summer of 1995 was eye-opening on many levels, but the thing I remembered most was the inescapable military presence. When I went to the mall because the airline had lost my luggage, I saw soldiers around every corner. It was hard to concentrate on finding underwear with so many machine guns around. I remember a teenage girl laughing with her friends outside a store. She could have been any teenybopper, except she accessorized with an Uzi. The most disconcerting thing was that this was normal for them. We drove past a McDonald's on our way to the Dead Sea and there were four military Humvees out front, as if Ronald McDonald himself were under siege. I couldn't imagine living like that every day.

Looking at the tanks in Battery Park, my eyes drifted upward to a giant billboard of a man's face towering above the barbed-wire fence. Calm and omniscient, looking down over all the military might, FDR offered one simple message: Think Different. I couldn't stop staring. Franklin Delano Roosevelt—the man who'd been president when Pearl Harbor was attacked and when the United States entered World War II—was now floating high above the evidence of our military reaction, telling us to think different. But he was speaking on behalf of Apple, the paragon of American consumerism. It was kind of a mind fuck. Yet it somehow said everything about what we were doing as a country. We were responding to a religious attack with military might and consumerism. Framing the events of 9/11 as an attack on our way of life, President George W. Bush told us to do our part and keep shopping; the military would protect us from the evildoers.

The next day, the observation deck at the Empire State Building reopened. Looking out over New York City's marred skyline, I couldn't shake the feeling that our government's response was wrong. Not only wrong, but destructive. The people who had wreaked such physical and emotional damage on the United States were not stupid—they were fundamentalists on a mission. Something I knew more than a little bit about.

Not too many years earlier I'd ranted about the horrors of abortion to anyone who would listen, believing we should do whatever it took to stop the immoral taking of innocent lives. I never condoned violence, but I'd been aware that a small group of fundamentalists did. They bombed abortion clinics and killed doctors, justifying their actions as part of a war to save the unborn. These people believed it was their responsibility to do something about the fact that a baby was dying every twenty seconds in America—even if that meant killing people. How was that different than the terrorists behind the 9/11 attacks who believed it was their duty to take action against what they saw as an oppressive force killing their families and friends? Both were extremist reactions born out of religious fundamentalism.

I left the Empire State Building, my mind reeling. I was a geek. I sat in front of computers all day looking for patterns. But the conclusions I had drawn on the observation deck were incredibly disturbing. If the world of Christian fundamentalism was not all that different from Islamic fundamentalism, if fundamentalism was fundamentalism and terrorism sometimes grew out of it, then it was not inconceivable—given the way I'd been raised—that I could have been a suicide bomber if I'd been born in Iran or Pakistan or Saudi Arabia. It was an utterly terrifying thought. I hadn't thought about God or country in so long. Was fundamentalism itself bad? Was I still a fundamentalist? It was too overwhelming to think about, so I decided to go get wasted and dance with a bunch of goths.

Heads turned when I walked into the Batcave, not because of my oh-so-sexy pale skin and death-warmed-over look, but because the goths are an insular group, and I was clearly an outsider. I ordered a Red Bull and vodka. Then another. And finally, for the first time in my life, I stepped on a dance floor and danced. For hours. I was tall enough—and drunk enough—to spin the disco ball above all our heads, a dancing giant fascinated by the drops of light spilling over waves of darkness. I fell asleep on the couch right next to the dance floor with the knowledge that my world had been turned upside down. I dreamed of swaying pine trees.

I woke up to a bouncer prodding me. I stumbled onto Thirtieth Street and wandered deliriously toward Hell's Kitchen.

When I got back to L.A., I quit my job.

Googling for God

I hadn't seen my family in three years. After my mom died, we stopped celebrating the holidays. No Thanksgiving, no Christmas—nothing. I went to visit them once in 1999 but, obsessed with my work and being successful, I hadn't seen them since. So when I finally visited Plano, Texas, in early 2002 I was shocked by what I found. My dad was in a deep depression, devastated by losing my mom and pissed at God for destroying his family. The girls, now eighteen and nineteen, were living together and in a lot of trouble. It was a mess. My sister Kristen was arrested for drug possession during my visit, and I decided, like the good conservative I was, that I would help her to help herself. We set up a bond agreement that she would pay off every month and I went back to California, shaken by the depth of my family's collapse. Why would God do this to us?

It had been years since I'd really thought of Him. I'd never questioned God's existence, just like I'd never questioned my parents, teachers, preachers or friends who taught me about Him. But the world was in shambles because of fundamentalism, and my family was in shambles because God had taken my mom from us. Did God even exist? Because if he did, he was an asshole.

I needed some facts and, most of all, I needed to know where I stood. The litmus test of being a good Christian in my family was your belief in the inerrancy of the Bible and your political activism; God and country, inextricably linked. I'd been to church once since my mom died and hadn't been politically active since the Fourth of July service at Thomas Road. So, was I still a fundamentalist? Was I even still a Christian?

Every summer when I was a kid, our teachers assigned us a Bible passage to memorize before the fall. Whoever recited the passages perfectly on the first day of school earned a trip to the water park. The entire foundation of my fundamentalist Christian upbringing centered on the Bible being the inerrant word of God; my parents always said that most "Christians" weren't really Christians because they didn't follow the word of God literally, word for word. So I was all about the memorizing thing. Almost none of the other students would memorize the passages, but I always did, and each September, I impressed the teachers with my perfect recitations. Sermon on the Mount, Psalm 23, John 10—I could do them all. The only thing better than missing school to go to the water slides when the lines were empty, was doing it in Jesus' name.

In Sunday school and Bible study it had been a given that the Bible was created when God spoke to a few very special humans who wrote down exactly what he'd said, word for word. It was the cornerstone of my faith; my family's requirement for any church we might attend was that they affirm the inerrancy of the Bible. So after years of building search engines, I decided to finally use them to do a little research of my own. The inerrant Word of God seemed like a good place to start. I googled "who wrote the Bible" and learned that there were no actual scripts from Jesus' time, that the authors of the four Gospels never knew Jesus, none of the Gospels were written down until at least forty years after Jesus' death, and that people continued to revise the scripts for at least a hundred years afterward.

It took me a while to get my head around what I'd discovered: The New Testament was created from oral testimony and was written and revised by multiple authors over many decades. Basically, The Bible was a giant game of telephone—played thousands of years before telephones existed.

Next I found out that there were a bunch of Gospels that hadn't been included in the Bible. The collection even had a badass name—the Apocrypha. All those many years of memorizing and studying and discussing the Bible, and no one thought it was important to mention that there were other writings about Jesus that weren't in the Bible? That at some point many years after Jesus' time, a group of guys sat around a table and decided what should or shouldn't be in the good book? That they had decided what the inerrant word of God was? What could possibly be in the Apocrypha that I hadn't been allowed to read? My life operating system was based on a first-century urban legend edited by a bunch of self-serving aristocrats hundreds of years later. This was the Greatest Lie of Omission Ever Told. It was time for an upgrade.

Lone Star

My sister Kristen almost never called me. So when she called and told me she needed my help, I flew out the next day. I landed in Dallas, thinking she was home in Plano, but she was actually in Austin trying to get away from her "friends." She picked me up and we spent the two-hundred-mile ride back to Austin talking. The picture Kristen painted of her life was grim: she was addicted to speed, couldn't get a proper job, and was broke. We arrived at her "place," a motel she rented by the week, early the following morning, and I began thinking up another plan to help her help herself. A few hours later, she went to get breakfast and I heard the worst sound any brother could ever hear—my baby sister screaming at the top of her lungs. I raced outside just in time to see Kristen being cuffed and wrestled into the backseat of a police car. She kept yelling to me over her shoulder that she hadn't done anything wrong. And then she was gone. I stood, in a total daze and watched the cop car drive away. I had no idea where she was being taken or how to find her. I didn't even know where I was. So I called my best friend Ramin and asked him to figure out where the hell I was and to find me the best criminal-defense lawyer in Tarrant County—the one who played golf with the judges.

I knew Kristen had been paying her bail

and had no drugs in her possession, so why she'd been arrested was a total mystery. I called the local police department and they couldn't tell me where she was. I started to panic. If I didn't figure out what was going on, Kristen was going to spend the night in jail. It took hours, but I finally learned that she was in the Austin City Jail. After racing there, the officers told me that they were holding her for the officials in Plano and couldn't release her under any circumstances. And I couldn't see her. So I drove three and a half hours to Plano and learned that they had a warrant out for her arrest because her bail had been pulled. There was nothing I could do that night. I headed back toward Austin and tried to sleep for a few hours at a motel. Instead of sleeping I was sick the whole time imagining what she was going through, alone and afraid.

The next day I figured out that Kristen had been the victim of a bail-bond scam. She'd been paying off her bond on time every month—part of why she was still broke—and was about to make her last payment. But, instead of allowing her to do that, her bail bondsman had pulled it so he would get all his money back, leaving Kristen broke and in jail. Then he could go back to her and have her pay him again, which she would have to do in order to get out. When I finally got in touch with the guy, he tried to get me to put her back on a payment plan. That's when I realized my plan to help her help herself had failed—and would fail again. Alone, Kristen would end up going back to this asshole or someone else like him who would only extort her for more money. I saw in an instant the entire market built on taking advantage of desperate people like my sister, preying on the poor and fueling their downward spirals.

Like any good conservative, I'd grown up believing in the twin virtues of rugged individualism and self-reliance. But the idea that Kristen could just pull herself up "by her bootstraps" was absurd. These were great concepts, but they made no sense in real life. I knew that she wouldn't be able to get back on her feet without help from other people—in this case, me and a lawyer. And somehow Ramin found the one lawyer who really did play golf with all the Tarrant County judges. We met, and I asked him to get her out of jail and let me take her out of state, away from all her druggie friends. He said he could do it, for four thousand dollars. It took another day and a half, more drives between Austin and Plano, and a maze of bureaucratic hell, but the lawyer got the judge to agree, and on the third day, she was finally released. When she came out and saw me she started crying. As we hugged I said, "We are going to California—right now." She jumped in the car.

After a two-day drive, we got to my apartment in downtown L.A. Kristen moved in with me, kicked drugs cold turkey, and started to piece her life back together. And I ditched conservatism.

Heresy

As a young boy, I had a big epiphany one day and told my parents that God had to exist because he had to start everything. They both smiled widely and congratulated me for my brilliance. Was creationism a fairy tale, too? I began looking at alternatives for how the universe could have been created. As it turned out, a lot of people had been asking similar questions and were working diligently to figure it out in an obscure little field known as science.

Who knew? I was amazed by my first field trip to the foreign land of scientific inquiry. Facts were substantiated and theories were declared as such. My favorite theory postulated that universes might just come into existence from time to time via forces we don't yet understand. Emergent behavior, which posited that a number of elements acting independently sometimes create unpredictable effects, made a lot of sense to me, since that's basically how the internet evolved. What was most comforting, though, was that there wasn't one definitive answer; there were plenty of ways that the universe could have happened that seemed significantly more plausible than a glorified children's story about six days and an earthling named Adam.

But what about human beings? Life didn't just start on earth by itself. God had to have made it—there were zebras and insects and a bunch of weird stuff in the oceans. That all had to come from somewhere, right? But scientists had looked into that, too, and, though it was a dirty word in my house, evolution kind of made sense to me. I learned about self-replicating molecules and mutation and natural selection. So this was how humans had come to exist on earth; a perfect example of emergent behavior. My dad had always said that God must have created the world because it was so amazing. But I saw the opposite—there was no way someone or something could have conjured up all that amazingness. It made much more sense that, like I'd seen with the birth and development of the internet, gazillions of independent actions kept colliding over and over again, generating unpredictable results.

I'd needed to know if there was a factual reason that God had to exist. And there wasn't. Everything—the universe, the earth, animals, human beings—could have been created without God. So twenty years after my first epiphany, I had another one: It's all just one big coincidence. Now, everything made sense to me—and the burden I didn't know I'd been carrying since August 25, 1996, lifted. It wasn't my fault that my mom had died. Taking her and leaving me wasn't some inscrutable part of God's plan—it was just random. There was no comfort in thinking God had a reason to sacrifice my mom, but it was incredibly comforting to know that sometimes bad shit just happens.

Getting rid of God filled me with an incredible sense of peace. The terrible recurring nightmares about my mom stopped. I could get on with my life, because I knew who I was. I wasn't a fundamentalist or a conservative or even a Christian.

I was an atheist.

SILENT ALL THESE YEARS

In early 2003, my dad called me and said he was moving to Newport Beach, California—and he wanted me and Kristen to move in with him. Live with my dad? No way! But maybe this was a chance to heal the wounds that had formed in his relationship with Kristen—and to help my dad come out of his depression. Plus, the air would be cleaner in Newport Beach. I'd had pneumonia a few times and couldn't figure out what was going on. Thinking maybe it had something to do with the conditions in my apartment, I headed down to Orange County with Kristen.

It was weird to be in the same house as my dad again. Religion wasn't a part of either of our lives anymore, and because neither of us was technically working, though I was blogging and coding, we sat together and talked about the news. As the War on Terror heated up, I was reminded daily that, though I was no longer a Christian, a lot of people in the United States—including many of those holding important leadership positions in the country— were. As our leaders frothed at the mouth with the rhetoric of war, I could see the secret fundamentalist references hidden in some of the propaganda. For the first time in years, I was captivated by politics.

George W. Bush's response to 9/11 had deeply troubled me since my trip to New York. I understood the logic behind targeting Al Qaeda in Afghanistan, but the blaring, non-stop U.S. nationalism didn't sit well with me. I spent a lot of time on Metafilter, the first community blog, where thousands of people were posting in an attempt to figure out what was going on in our country. Many online conversations centered on the context surrounding Al Qaeda—figuring out who they were, what they wanted, and why they wanted it. As the Bush administration laid the foundation for an invasion of Iraq and the mainstream media aired nothing but support, people online were openly skeptical. Al Qaeda was not based in Iraq, none of the 9/11 terrorists were in or from Iraq, and UN inspectors had concluded Iraq had no WMDs. Invading Iraq was inexplicable both from a tactical and a strategic standpoint. The people online were looking at it from a secular point of view and were baffled. There was no logical reason for the invasion. I realized the invasion of Iraq would never make sense from a secular point of view. But it made perfect sense from a religious one.

The focus on WMDs was a cover. No one was talking about the obvious fact that a Christian country, led by a born-again Christian, was about to attack a Muslim country. If I'd still been a Christian fundamentalist, I would have enlisted right then. This was the greatest opportunity to further the kingdom of God since the Crusades. The hard-core Christians knew exactly what was going on. And so did the Muslim world. Though she was scathingly criticized for saying it, Ann Coulter was the only one with the balls to say what Christian fundamentalists were thinking. A few days after 9/11, she wrote, "We should invade their countries, kill their leaders and convert them to Christianity." A year later, Jerry Falwell called the prophet Muhammad a "terrorist" on *60 Minutes*. This sparked riots in the Middle East and resulted in a Muslim cleric calling for his death. And now, George W. Bush was about to give Osama bin Laden exactly what he wanted: an unprovoked holy war in the Middle East. It was off-the-charts insane.

In early February 2003, my dad and I watched as Colin Powell spoke to the United Nations. When his speech was over, we looked at each other and didn't say a word. It was really going to happen. A month later, Howard Dean gave a fiery speech at the California Democratic Party convention, criticizing the party for its response to the war. Video of his speech went viral on Metafilter and all the political blogs just as Bush's war rhetoric was ratcheting up. Four days later, on March 19, 2003, the United States started dropping bombs on Baghdad.

The war on Iraq had begun.

The Heart is a Battlefield

When my mom was dying, she asked my dad for a tape recorder so she could leave her last words for each of us. My sisters and I had never heard the tapes, but we knew they were in a box of my mom's things that Dad had never been able to open. While he and Kristen were out one day, I decided to find them. I knew there were a bunch of boxes in his closet, so I snuck in and carefully opened each of them until I found the right one. The box contained her wedding ring, two unlabeled tapes, a few three-by-five note cards, and my parents' wedding photos. My mom was so beautiful in the photographs, and their love was as evident as I remembered it from my childhood. I carefully put everything else back and took the cassettes with me.

A few days later, I bought a tape player at Target and waited for Dad and Kristen to leave. As soon as they were gone, I started listening. The first cassette didn't have anything on it—I fast-forwarded and rewound it, but it was blank. The second one had Mom's voice. I hadn't heard her voice in nearly ten years, but I could tell her message was for my dad, so I didn't listen. I fast-forwarded to see if there was something for me later in the tape, but there wasn't. Disappointed, I returned the tapes to their place in the box. But as I replaced them, I saw the three-by-five cards and pulled them out. One of them said "Jimmy" on it. My heart lurched. After a minute I started reading, the card trembling in my hand. I can't remember what the first part said because of what was at the end. The very last thing my dying mother had written to me was, "Your heart will be a battlefield for Satan."

Holy. Shit.

For years I'd been ignoring the gnawing fear that my mom would be horrified that I wasn't being a good Christian—and that was even before I became an atheist. I knew how badly she wanted me to succeed, so I'd focused solely on that—and on proving that dropping out of college wouldn't ruin my life. But being a good person was more important to her than worldly success, and I knew it. Her note was a stark reminder of how far I'd strayed from her beliefs. I had to prove to her—and to myself— that I could be an atheist and still be a moral person.

My mom's moral code centered on one thing: truth. She hated lying in any form and believed we had a moral obligation to tell the truth, even when it was inconvenient or un- comfortable to do so. She'd done this herself many times, even as a high school student.

There was the famous story in my family of when she stood up against doctoring the stats in her Junior Achievement program, even though everyone hated her as a result. The Iraq War was being waged in the name of her beliefs, and it was based on lies. This was my chance to fight for truth. I was under no illusions that I could really change anything, but if I looked back on this moment in ten years and saw that I hadn't done everything I could have, I wouldn't be able to live with myself. So I had to help stop the war.

A few days later, I stumbled on an op-ed by Thom Hartmann "How to Take Back America," an impassioned plea to those opposing the war. He made a persuasive case for antiwar activists to take over the Democratic Party. Structurally, there was no way a third party could ever win, so the only viable option to stopping the war was to elect an antiwar Democrat who could beat Bush in the 2004 election. I knew he was right. Howard Dean seemed like the best bet—in addition to being staunchly antiwar, he was a doctor and a centrist. He had balanced the budget when he was the governor of Vermont, and like me, he believed that health care was the United States' number-one priority. So I decided to register as—gasp!—a Democrat and to support Dean in the Democratic primary.

Orange County was not known as a Democratic stronghold, so I tried my best to get involved where I could. I went to a Young Democrats meeting and did some voter registration, but I was unimpressed. Then some of the bloggers supporting Dean started using a new internet tool called Meetup, which helped online communities connect offline. There were groups for knitters and hikers and pub crawlers. It was the fastest way for Dean's supporters to meet and organize. The campaign saw this grassroots upswell and began officially promoting the Howard Dean Meetups nationally. It became a phenomenon.

On April 2, 2003, I went to the Diedrich Coffee shop in the Irvine Spectrum Center for one of the first ever Meetups. Fifty strangers, thrown together by the internet, met among throngs of teenagers shuttling between Hot Topic and Forever 21. We stared at each other, no one quite sure what we were supposed to do. Finally, we went around the room and introduced ourselves. I told everyone that I had never voted before, but that I'd just registered as a Democrat so that I could vote for Dean because we had to stop the war. I was applauded. My story caught the attention of a woman named Maggie who asked if she could quote me for her blog. I told her I'd blogged about it already, and the next day she commented on my post. We became fast friends and it wasn't long before we formed an offshoot of the Orange County Howard Dean Meetup just for geeks.

The online base of operations for the antiwar movement was MoveOn.org. Everyone was trying to understand what was going on in the country and why the media wasn't telling us the real story, so MoveOn.org sent out an email pitching the "Great MoveOn Interview." The idea was to match two people from the same area code and have them interview each other for an hour. They would report back what the other person said, and then MoveOn.org would do some fancy linguistic analysis that would miraculously figure out how the media each person consumed affected the way he or she talked about the war—or something like that. I thought it was brilliant, so I signed up, and because I lived in Los Angeles, I was paired with a Hollywood producer named David Blocker. We had a great conversation and he subscribed to my blog. A month later, he forwarded me an email from another producer, Robert Greenwald. Robert needed a researcher for a few months who "didn't need to be paid very much." I searched his name on IMDb and found out that he'd made dozens of television movies and miniseries featuring such icons as Farrah Fawcett and Sally Field. But when I saw that he'd executive produced *Unprecedented*, a documentary about the 2000 presidential election that I'd seen just a few months before, I knew I wanted the job.

Crucify the Insincere

The next day I met with Robert at his office, which was a converted motel in the shadow of the giant Sony Pictures Studio lot in Culver City. He was deeply troubled about what was happening in Iraq and immediately started pitching me his idea for a film. Despite the Bush administration's ten-month propaganda campaign to convince Americans that Iraq had WMDs, no nuclear weapons or even chemical weapons had been found. It was July 2003.

The administration was now saying that Iraq had nuclear programs. But as Robert reminded me, "a program can be just a piece of paper!" An article online by former CIA analyst Ray McGovern had caught his eye and after talking with Ray, Robert learned that there were a lot of credible insiders who wanted to go on the record with the truth. So Robert's plan was to make a documentary showing how the government's weapons-of-mass-destruction language kept shifting, exposing the lie that the mainstream media was ignoring—as fast as humanly possible, so we could end the occupation. Was I in? Hell yeah.

I got to work researching and documenting every statement about WMDs by government officials. I had to put them in chronological order with the original transcript for context and then cross-reference them with the facts. It should have been an exceedingly boring task, but it felt like the most important thing I'd ever done. The final document was one hundred pages long, with another thousand pages of transcripts. I knew exactly when each quote had been said, who had said it, where the person had said it, whether the news reports had interpreted it in the right context, and who owned the footage. I triple-checked everything; I was determined to get it all exactly right. I drove back and forth between Newport Beach and L.A. daily. The whole thing—the all-nighters, the large quantities of Mountain Dew, the nights spent under my desk in a sleeping bag—felt like my internet start-up days. None of us knew if anyone would ever actually see the film. The whole reason we were making it was because the mainstream media wouldn't cover the story, so we knew it definitely wasn't going to air on NBC or PBS. But there was no time to dwell on that. We had to move fast.

My biggest challenge was getting the actual video footage. Without it, my research was useless. I could get clips either from news programs or official government sources, but news programs charged a lot and took a while, and government sources, while they gave the clips for free, took forever. Even a few days was too long for me to wait, so I investigated ways to save the streams from the White House and C-SPAN websites. If I could save the streams, I should be able to copy the footage into our new editing software, Final Cut Pro. We'd be able to start editing with the low-quality streams right away, then swap it for the higher-quality footage whenever I received it. But the video-streaming technologies at the time were designed for companies that wanted to prevent people like me from downloading the videos and copying them. I fired up a packet sniffer to figure out the URL of the stream and then found an obscure shareware program that would save the file. No software could convert that into something Final Cut would accept, so I brought my home computer into the office, hooked it up to a video-output box and then played all the streams onto VHS tapes, which were then digitized into Final Cut. Rube Goldberg would have been proud.

With my hacked-together pirating machine (barely) working, we finished the film in four months. Because we couldn't go through normal media channels, we had to get creative with the film's distribution. So we partnered with MoveOn.org and the Center for American Progress, a brand-new liberal think tank, to create an alternate distribution model based on the internet—and people. On November 3, 2003, MoveOn.org sent an email asking its members to donate thirty dollars toward an anti-Bush ad campaign. In return, they'd receive a copy of our movie, *Uncovered: The Whole Truth About the*

Iraq War. None of us knew how many copies we would sell, so we printed five thousand and hoped we'd sell at least half. An hour after the email went out, Robert got an email from Wes Boyd at MoveOn.org saying we had already sold out. Within two days, we had sold thirty thousand copies and raised nearly a million dollars. I felt like I'd just witnessed a miracle. My dad called to congratulate me and asked if he could take me to lunch. I said yes, unaware that he had some big news of his own.

Back in May, I'd dragged my dad to my second Dean Meetup, and was happy when he decided to keep going to them. Thrilled that my dad was taking such an interest, I didn't catch on to the real reason until he told me that he'd asked my friend Maggie on a date. Obsessed with work and rarely at home, I hadn't paid much attention to their developing relationship. So I was pretty dumbfounded when, over some chips and guacamole, my dad told me that he and Maggie were getting married in December. As in, the month after the one we were currently in. What!? My dad had been in one relationship since my mom died, but it hadn't been serious. I was shocked and a little bit worried. I asked him if he was sure—they hadn't known each other that long! But he said when he knew, he knew; it had been that way with my mom, too. That's when I saw in his eyes what I'd missed over the past few months: he was happy.

Our first theatrical screening of *Uncovered* was on November 11, 2003, at the Laemmle Theater in Santa Monica. When I drove up to park, there was a huge line all the way down the street outside the theater. Robert was upset that we had scheduled our screening at the same time as some big movie premiere. But the big movie premiere turned out to be ours! Starving for answers about the war, people had come out in droves. There was so much demand that we moved the screening into the biggest theater they had, and scheduled another one for later that night. People waited outside during the entire first screening for a chance to see it during the second screening. We even had a few protesters. Watching the film I had poured my heart into with over five hundred people, including my dad, Maggie, and Ramin, was the greatest experience I'd ever had. When I worked at Lycos and Business.com, I had built sites that millions of people used, but I had never sat in a room full of people while they laughed and booed and yelled at something I had helped create. It was exhilarating.

After selling thirty thousand DVDs, we had what Robert liked to call a "high-class problem" because we didn't actually have thirty thousand DVDs. It would take a month to make them, but people didn't want to wait. We shipped out the five thousand we had, and then MoveOn.org came up with the brilliant idea to ask the people who already had DVDs to host screenings. They could register their screening on the website, and anyone could punch in a zip code and find one nearby. By the next week, over two thousand screenings had happened all over the world, and more than a million people had seen the film.

The last time I'd felt that high was when thousands of volunteers were connected through the Open Directory Project. But this was so much more meaningful because the cause was so much more important. People organizing over the internet were able to do what multibillion-dollar media conglomerates and the most prestigious newspapers in the world could not—expose the lies behind the Bush administration's invasion of Iraq to the world. We were going to stop the war!

On December 19, my dad and Maggie got married. It was a simple ceremony at the Orange County courthouse. My whole family was there, together again, happy. I looked at the friend who was now my stepmother, and realized that she was in my life, in my sisters' lives, in my dad's life because of one thing. People connecting through the internet.

Some People Say

I wasn't the only one intoxicated by our success. Everyone who'd worked on *Uncovered* wanted to do it again, and the next project wasn't hard to find. Throughout production, we had marveled at the disaster that was the mainstream media. At first we couldn't understand how they consistently got everything wrong, but eventually the problem became obvious. The administration's unofficial cheerleader, Fox News, kept calling anyone who contradicted the White House or the Pentagon a traitor. If someone went on TV and questioned the Bush administration's position, the person was silenced and ostracized. Meanwhile, all the other networks were busy mimicking Fox, trying to capture a share of its sky-high ratings. Fox was a virus infecting the media and the public. If we didn't do something, Fox News would remain the unchecked mouthpiece for the Republican Party, Bush would almost be guaranteed to win reelection, and there'd be no hope of stopping the war. We had found the target of our next documentary. And I'd found a girlfriend. So I moved from Newport Beach to Los Angeles to be closer to her and to eliminate my commute.

It was my job to find usable footage, which was complicated by the fact that we couldn't get it from Fox. So we set up a half dozen TiVos to record Fox 24/7, but who was going to watch Fox twenty-four hours a day? MoveOn.org sent an email to its most active members asking if any of them would be willing to watch and report back to us what they found. About twenty-five people—most of them over the age of fifty—signed up to work in shifts around the clock. Because the most important thing was what the reporters were saying, I wanted to experiment with saving the closed-captioning on the live feed so we could search for key words in the transcripts. This would make it possible both to identify patterns and to find clips. It ended up being one of our most potent weapons and helped our volunteer watchers discover some of Fox's favorite phrases. My personal favorite was "some people say." Whenever a Fox News personality wanted to insert some idea without sourcing it, he or she would preface the Republican talking point with the phrase "some people say." Once those magic words were uttered, there was no need to offer facts or evidence. We found the phrase hundreds of times in our transcripts, and it became one of the funniest parts of the film.

We produced *Outfoxed: Rupert Murdoch's War on Journalism* in total secrecy, hoping to surprise the media. Our premiere was in New York and I boarded the airplane wondering how it would be received and if anyone would even care. I was the most optimistic one on our team, because I knew that there was nothing the media loved more than talking about the media, so I figured we'd draw plenty of attention. I flew out on JetBlue, the new airline touting live television in-flight. A few hours into the trip, I was flipping through the channels and literally jumped out of my seat. There, on MSNBC talking to Keith Olbermann, was Robert! When I had boarded the airplane no one had even known that the film existed; now its existence was being broadcast on television? Once I landed at JFK, I found out that, just a few minutes after I left for the airport, *The New York Times* had asked Fox News for a comment on our film for a feature story embargoed until the movie's release the next day. Olbermann had just left Fox, was still tuned in to the gossip mill, and couldn't wait to stick it to his former employer. MSNBC called Robert, and a few hours later, he was filming in the network's L.A. studio. It was wild, but it was a precursor for the attention that the movie would generate. Now the premiere was a big deal and our press conference the next morning was filled with media outlets, including Fox News, which had sent one of its reporters, Eric Shawn. He gave us our money quote: "it's unfair, it's slanted, and it's a hit job. And I haven't even seen it yet." I immediately put it on the website. We held our breath for the next few weeks to see if Fox would sue us for using the footage without its permission but, presumably afraid of more attention, they never did.

After the premiere I finally relaxed and re-alized almost immediately that I wasn't feeling quite right. I'd moved into a new apartment a few weeks earlier, and noticed that I was getting winded going up the stairs. I went to a holistic doctor who put me on a strict diet of lean meat and vegetables, and I forgot about it. We did house screenings again, and even had a small theatrical release of *Outfoxed*. *Fahrenheit 9/11* had just been released, and a lot of people were in the mood to watch lefty documentaries. Unlike *Uncovered*, *Outfoxed* was a lot of fun, and became a big hit. I analyzed LexisNexis and found that there were three times as many stories connecting Republicans with Fox News after the release of our film. We were changing the misperception that Fox News was "fair and balanced," and we were helping to stop other news outlets from copying them. We started to see our films as a way to influence the larger media narrative; how many people saw them was actually less important than their effect on the broader public dialogue. I'd loved hacking BBSes and the internet, but now I was hacking the media. Being an activist was addictive, and it was exhilarating to cause so much trouble for the bad guys. It was geek crack.

And then we lost the election. I'd been invited to the Frontline Club to talk about the film, which is why I was drinking beer at a bar in London with Greenpeace activists at six a.m.

the day after the election. Everyone else was depressed, but I was too much in shock to feel anything. I just couldn't believe it. We all knew that Kerry was a shitty candidate, but how the hell had this happened? People had the correct information! We'd given it to them! We'd exposed the lies, but people didn't care. They had still reelected Bush. I was crushed and disoriented and not accustomed to failure. I'd believed that if we uncovered the truth about the war, the American people would do the right thing. But they hadn't.

I returned to the United States shaken. I started working on a new documentary, but my heart wasn't in it. We hadn't stopped the war. We'd failed. Plus, I couldn't really breathe. It had become harder and harder to walk up the hill to my car from my girlfriend's apartment. I was also having doubts about my relationship and I agreed to see a therapist with her to try and work it out. The therapist, ever concerned with "being present," made us read a stupid book on mindfulness. What became clear in a relatively short amount of time—in addition to the fact that wherever I went, there I was—was that I was sick and not doing anything about it. When our therapist asked me why I was ignoring the fact that I couldn't breathe, I realized it was because I didn't want to know the reason. Which was stupid. So I made an appointment to see a pulmonologist on the following Monday. And I didn't know why, but I suddenly knew that I had to break up with my girlfriend right away.

THE LONG WAY AROUND

Dr. Stanley Kahan took one look at me and asked who'd referred me. I told him no one; he was just the closest pulmonary specialist to my office covered by my insurance. Pause. "Uh, so you just came off the street?" he asked. "Yeah," I said. He was flummoxed by my nonchalance. He immediately did a pulmonary-function test, which revealed that my lung capacity was 25 percent of what it should be. Sometimes doctors don't tell you things straight, but Dr. Kahan told me in no uncertain terms that I had to stop being an idiot and make this my number-one priority. My lungs were obviously a mess for a reason, so he ordered a CT scan and X-ray. I came back for my results a few days later, and Dr. Kahan told me I had restricted lung disease due to scarring. What he didn't know was what was causing it or if it could be stopped. In my case, it was most likely caused by one of the three things that had saved my life: chemotherapy, radiation, or the bone-marrow transplant. To learn more he had to do a biopsy on the scar tissue.

I got the results from the biopsy on August 11. They weren't good. They'd found that the problem was radiation fibrosis—untreatable scarring of the lungs due to radiation. It was late onset and progressing slowly, yet steadily. But that clearly wasn't the whole story. Only 40 percent of my lungs were scarred, so I should have had 60 percent capacity, not 25 percent. Dr. Kahan needed another biopsy of the scar tissue to locate the source of the additional restriction. He was hoping to find and diagnose something he could treat. He told me that his goal was to get me to a place where I could function, and he mentioned that I might be a good candidate for a lung transplant. Wait, as in . . . replace my lungs with someone else's?!

When I got back to work I immediately googled lung-transplant survival rates and learned that 87.8 percent of people make it three months, 76 percent make it a year, 54 percent make it three years, and 39 percent make it five years. I learned that people recommended for lung transplants have life expectancies of two years or less. Two years?! I'd had no idea I was that close to death. Before completely panicking, I called Dr. Kahan and asked how long he thought I had. Like all doctors, he hesitated to throw out specific numbers, but said it was definitely less than twenty years. I knew with some certainty that I was going to die young.

UCLA Surgeons are Pussies

The next lung biopsy was a disaster. The first one had been noninvasive, but this biopsy would be a real surgery at a real hospital, Brotman Medical Center. The surgeon had to cut open my chest to extract a piece of lung tissue. Several days after the procedure, as I was walking out of my hospital room to go home, the right side of my chest started bubbling out like a balloon. It turned out that the surgeon had nicked a piece of my lung and I was bleeding internally. They stopped the bleeding, but I now had a hole in my lung and could no longer function without an oxygen machine. When

I was released, I went to Newport Beach with Dad and Maggie to recover. That night, an oxygen machine accompanied by a dozen tanks of pure O2 arrived. The plastic tubing I stuck up my nose felt like shackles. I did not want to stay in Newport Beach, and I desperately tried to come up with a scenario in which it would be possible for me to remain independent, but by morning it was obvious that I could not live on my own. On September 6, Dr. Kahan called with the biopsy results. There was nothing to treat. My lungs were wrecked and I needed a transplant.

We quickly learned that lungs are an extremely scarce resource, and that there's a rigorous process for getting on the waiting list. Everyone was trying to figure out some reason to not put me on, and the reason to deny me was painfully obvious: I was a cancer survivor. For my body to accept new lungs, my immune system would have to be suppressed, which, because of my history, would leave me open to infections and tumors. If I got cancer again, I would certainly die and the precious lungs would be wasted. The odds of getting on the list were not in my favor. So I had to get to work.

There were three hospitals in the area with lung-transplant programs, UCLA, USC, and Cedars-Sinai. I pored over the publicly available statistics and found that UCLA had the best survival rates. They also performed more transplants than anyone else, because they had a special technique to revive lungs that were too damaged for other hospitals to use. As a result, they did sixty lung transplants a year while Cedars-Sinai did five. If I were on the list at UCLA, there would be a much greater chance of getting a transplant in time. But on September 26, I got a call from the appointment scheduler at UCLA's heart- and lung-transplant program. They wouldn't see me, and the scheduler couldn't tell me why. Maggie was livid and needed answers. She kept calling until she found out that I'd been denied because the extensive scarring in my upper chest made the surgery too difficult. I was pissed. So I blogged about it.

My friends and family were outraged when they saw my post. Ellen, one of the *Outfoxed* volunteers, wrote a scathing email to UCLA, which prompted my sister Kelly and others to do the same. They accused UCLA of declining the "difficult" cases to minimize its risk of failure in order to keep its success rates high.

I joked on my blog that I was going to register the domain uclasurgeonsarepussies.com. Everyone liked that. Meanwhile, Dr. Kahan, who had been consulting on my case since the beginning, started working on getting me into Cedars-Sinai.

A month later, I got a call from the very same UCLA scheduler who had initially told me that I'd been denied. She needed to set me up with a time to meet Dr. Joseph Lynch. I thought she was confused because I had already been rejected from the program, but she was adamant that I was on her list as needing an appointment. I had no idea what had happened, but I definitely wasn't going to try to convince her that it was a mistake!

Being accepted into the transplant program wasn't a guarantee that I'd get on the list—it only meant I was being considered for the list. I met with Dr. Lynch at the UCLA clinic and began the gauntlet that I would have to run over the next few months. There were tests and then more tests. There were meetings and then more meetings, all supervised by the delightful and ever-helpful insurance people. Everyone was trying to find a reason not to give me the lungs: UCLA because they didn't want to risk a bad transplant that would waste a lung and lower its numbers, and the insurance company because it would cost them a half-million dollars.

Finally, I was scheduled to meet with the head surgeon, Dr. Abbas Ardehali. At our meeting I asked him why I'd been rejected and then accepted to UCLA's program. As it turned out, the emails that Ellen, Kelly, and others had sent to a generic UCLA email account actually went somewhere, and had then been forwarded to Dr. Ardehali. He didn't like the accusation that UCLA surgeons were afraid to do tough surgeries. He was most certainly not a pussy. He was a bad motherfucker and wasn't about to let someone tell him what he couldn't do. So he overrode those refusing to see me and told them to get "the kid" in.

All my friends called in to put pressure on UCLA. Someone even called in as a documentary filmmaker following my story. My activist colleagues were not about to let them turn me down. But no one fought harder than Maggie. She yelled and cried on the phone, frequently at the same time. She started a blog, CheckOnJim.com. She wouldn't let up until she got results. Still, the transplant board was split. The opponents of giving me the transplant referenced the high likelihood that the cancer would come back, as well as the difficulty of the surgery itself. The scarring had wrapped around my lungs in such a way that the procedure would be incredibly complicated and there was a very real chance that I would die on the table. But the big positive was that I was young—most people needing lungs were much older—and otherwise healthy. My biggest advocate was Dr. Lynch, who officially recommended a double lung transplant. Most people on the transplant board—most importantly the medical director, Dr. David Ross, who was the one that had initially refused me—had never actually seen me. But Dr. Lynch had, and told them over and over again that I looked great, I just needed some new lungs. He fought them until they were convinced. In January 2006 I got a call from UCLA that I was on the list. My dad, Maggie, and Kristen were on their way home from a Chinese restaurant when I texted them the good news. Maggie called immediately and told me that my dad's fortune cookie had said, "Soon, you will witness a miracle."

Usually the process to get on the list takes just a couple of weeks, but it had been months for me, and I was getting sicker. I knew I didn't have much time, so I had to figure out what my chances were of actually getting the lungs before it was too late. The matching system between organ and recipient is a computer algorithm that takes into account a number of variables. For example, there could only be a five-hundred-mile radius between the lungs and UCLA, because they'd only have four hours to get them to me. But the biggest issue for me was that the lungs had to actually fit, which was complicated because I wasn't just insanely tall; I was also insanely thin. I started to run the numbers. I looked at the population statistics and calculated that if I were on the list at 6'5" it would take about nine years to get the lungs. I was 6'9". So my only shot at survival was if one of the Lakers happened to be an organ donor and suddenly dropped dead in a way that didn't damage his lungs. Statistically, I needed to exist in the computer as 6'2" or under to get the lungs in time. At my next appointment, I immediately asked what size lungs I was eligible for. And they said I was in the computer as eligible for donors who were 6'1" or taller. Relieved, I settled in to wait.

And then to wait some more.

The Call

I distracted myself for a year by making another movie. But by January 2007, I was down to 145 pounds, my lung capacity had dropped another 5 percent, and I was getting weaker and weaker. My fingertips were frequently numb, which was terrifying because it meant that I couldn't type as much—and that I had time to reflect.

I'd had a pretty crazy life. But after all the drama and successes and fighting and failures, there was only one thing that mattered to me: had I honored my mom with my life? The truth was, I couldn't really say yes. She'd always wanted me to be successful in life, and I'd figured out how to do that. She wanted me to be a moral person, so I'd fought against lies and tried to make the world a better place. But it didn't feel right. Something important was still missing.

I was nearing death. The transplant board

was worried. The doctors looked into why I hadn't been matched yet and saw that my height was in the computer as 6'5", not 6'1". They realized what I'd figured out a year earlier—that I would never get matched at that listed height—so they finally changed it to 5'11".

At 9:40 a.m. on Thursday, February 1, my phone rang. Then Maggie's phone rang. Then my dad's phone rang. It was time.

BREATHE

My dad is an annoyingly slow driver. Family legend has it that his only moving violation was for driving too slowly. He even slows down when the crosswalk countdown gets below five, so that he's perfectly positioned to stop when the light turns red. But that morning he flew through the carpool lane driving at the speed limit. It may have been the first time he ever drove above sixty miles per hour. When we screeched into the emergency-room parking area, the nurses were waiting to whisk me away for presurgery prep. It was 10:30 a.m.

As with the bone-marrow process, transplants are a highly coordinated event. That morning, UCLA had gotten a call from the

United Network for Organ Sharing (UNOS) to say that they might have a match for me. As soon as UCLA said they wanted the lungs, everything switched into motion. I was called to come in, and a doctor from UCLA was sent to get a visual on the lungs. During that time I would be prepped. If the doctor called back to say that the lungs looked good, I would be put under and the lungs would be put in a cooler and helicoptered to us. If the final check in the surgery room went well, they would cut me open and take out my failing breathing apparatus.

That was definitely going to be the tricky part. Because of all the scarring in my upper chest, my lungs were attached to my ribs. Which meant that Dr. Ardehali would be scraping them off, an obviously intricate and very dangerous process. Back when I'd had the lung biopsy, all they'd had to do was take out a little piece of my lung and they had nicked me. That hadn't been UCLA, of course, but still. This time they were actually going to scrape out my lungs. But the only thing that surpassed Dr. Ardehali's ego was his skill, so I put my faith in his hands.

Grace

No one but family is allowed in the presurgery prep area, so obviously all of my friends were there. Ramin, who is from Iran, got in by telling the staff he was my brother. All my documentary-film friends—so adept at being in places they weren't supposed to be—showed up. As I lay in bed with nurses hooking me up to things, signing papers and waiting for the lungs to arrive, we celebrated victory. It was literally standing room only as everyone huddled around my rolling bed trying not to get tangled in the curtains separating me from the other patients. Everyone had worked so hard for this moment. There was just one minor detail left.

That minor detail was etched across my dad's face. I could see he was excited, but the excitement was laced with anxiety. He knew that in a couple of hours a nurse would walk into the waiting room and tell him that the surgeons had stopped my heart. Not something any parent ever wants to hear. A machine would take over, pumping oxygen through my blood while Dr. Ardehali and his team swapped the lungs. The procedure would take three hours, and I knew my dad would be holding his breath the entire time. When they were done, the surgeons would turn off the machine, and then wait for the lungs to inflate . . . or not. I had seen this on television. I called it the money shot. I watched it over and over again, fascinated by the miracle of it. More than anyone else, I think my dad was aware that I either was going to breathe then or I would never breathe again.

At 12:30 p.m., the doctor who'd flown to check out the lungs called to say that they were good. He and the lungs were getting on the helicopter. I said quick goodbyes to everyone and was wheeled into surgery. They rolled me into the freezing room and plopped me down on the even colder table. There were cameras and tons of equipment and a bunch of strangers rushing around doing very important-looking things. When they finished hooking me up to a series of tubes, I knew it was only a matter of minutes before I was going to be put under.

Deathbed conversions have a special place in the hearts of Christians. Even if you have renounced God your entire life, your soul can be saved if you accept Jesus at the very end. It is an example of His grace. Rumors abound of famous nonbelievers turning to God in their final hours. Christians say that the nearness of death focuses and sharpens the mind, making the truth clear. That's totally what happened for me, minus the Jesus part.

Lying on the table in the center of a highly regimented whirlwind, I found myself strangely at peace. Gone were the sounds of the room. Gone was the freezing table beneath me. Gone was any fear of the surgery's outcome. There was only one thing I was aware of: the countless people who had gotten me to this moment. The friends who'd just been crowded around my hospital bed; the people who had emailed UCLA on my behalf; Maggie, who'd never stopped fighting for me; all the people who were blogging and advocating for me; and the nurses and surgeons, in whose hands I was placing my life. All these people—most of whom I didn't know and never would—had come together to save me, to give me life. I couldn't possibly deserve this. How could I ever repay this debt—a debt not of money but of life?

And that's when I truly found God.

God wasn't up in some mythical heaven. God was right there, talking to me, touching me, helping me—and blogging furiously in the waiting room.

God is just what happens when humanity is connected. And it was only by the grace of God—their grace—that I might be saved.

And in that, I had total faith.

REVELATIONS

I woke up twenty hours later. Standing before me were not the pearly gates of Heaven, but the coffee-stained teeth of my smiling father. We had done it. My heart was beating. I was, with the help of machines, breathing. I was alive.

Saved

Three different DNAs. Individually, they were useless, but together they equaled one functioning human. "Me." It was a miracle. I had been born again, by the grace of a connected humanity. But, as I learned over the next few months, connecting humanity isn't always grace-full. Figuring out how to get my body working again was the hardest thing I've ever done. Besides relearning how to breathe, I had to ensure that the three DNAs found peace with one another and didn't start a holy war in my body. It was painful. Often it seemed impossible. It was really, really messy. Kind of like everything else in the world.

It's one thing to believe in humanity connected. It's another to have humanity actually connected in your own body. I guess I'm pretty thick-headed, because it took turning my body into a mash-up for me to get it. Some part of me knew when I stole the computer out of my parents' room so I could get online. Some part of me knew when a stranger saved me with his bone marrow and a nurse risked her job to save my life. Some part of me knew when eighty thousand people came together to organize the web and when thousands of people came together to expose the lies of the Iraq War. Some part of me knew when my little sister needed help and when my dad found love again. But it took the collective gift of my family, friends, advocates, and doctors for me to truly understand. We are all connected, inextricably linked. We always have been, and now it is impossible for me to ignore.

I never understood why I would get so upset when people disrespected the internet. Yes, it was a tool to get things done, to connect people, and it was even sometimes a weapon to wield. But my whole life it felt like something more than that. After the lung transplant I finally got it. The internet illuminates what has always been—our interconnectedness. The internet is not a tool or a thing. It is how we communicate with God. It is sacred. Holy. All that time I thought I'd been far from God I wasn't. I'd been talking to God everyday for years—online. The internet saved me from the hell of Christian fundamentalism and the despair of atheism. And then it saved my life.

If God is humanity connected, then the internet is God incarnate; a manifestation of our connection, a rudimentary form of hyperconnected humanity.

Faith

When I was ten years old, sitting beside my dad watching him code, I noticed that there was one character he kept using over and over again. "What's that called?," I asked, pointing to the mysterious **#** above the 3 on the keyboard. "Some people call it the number sign, but I call it pound," he answered.

No one agrees on what to call **#** and no one really knows where it originated either; it just seems to have always existed. In the modern technological era, the octothorpe was first used to fill space on what would otherwise have been a blank button on the touchtone telephone. Today, hashtags are used to start something. You can put anything after **#** and what follows becomes a community, a movement, something that matters. It has become the symbol of the internet. For me, **#** is the symbol of a connected humanity. It represents my faith that people, connected, can create a new world.

It took me a while, but I finally figured out how I could truly honor my mom—how I could make her proud of me. What mattered most to her wasn't me going to college or getting married or having a great job. Yes, she wanted me to be a moral person. But what mattered most to her was simple. She wanted me to believe in God.

And I do.

I believe in **#**. I believe that we are God, the internet is our savior, and our purpose is to create the world we want. Each one of us is a creator. And together, we are The Creator.

#

All I know about the person whose lungs I now have is that he was twenty-two years old and six feet tall. I know nothing about who he was as a person, but I do know something about his family. I know that in the height of loss, when all any family should have to do is grieve, as their son, as their brother, lay motionless in bed, they were asked to give up to seven strangers a chance to live.

And they said yes.

Today I breathe through someone else's lungs while another's blood flows through my veins.

I have faith in people. I believe in God.

And the internet is my religion.

AFTERWORD

You have been given a very special gift—your life.

Most people spend that gift waiting. Waiting for a promotion, waiting for permission, waiting for a savior. But you can't wait. Life has no rollover minutes.

I used to believe there were many ways to sin. Now I believe that the real sin is wasting your life. Because it's not just *your* life. Everything we achieve is built on the contributions and sacrifices of others. It's our mom driving us to school, a friend loaning us rent money, an acquaintance introducing us to our future life partner. It's the farmers who grow the food we eat and the scientists who invent the cures that keep us alive. We are all connected, we are all in debt to each other, we all owe every moment of our lives to people we know—and to countless people we will never meet.

So what do we do? How do we pay back that debt?

Every one of us has a skill, a talent, a passion: something special and unique that no one else has. It's your purpose to figure out what that thing is and to contribute it to the world. And if you don't honor it—because school, or society, or your parents say you shouldn't— then you're wasting your gift.

When I left my dot-com job, I had no idea what I was meant to do. So I started saying yes to all the things I would normally say no to—especially the things that I was too shy to try. The more uncomfortable I felt, the more it meant that I needed to go for it. I started dancing, I went camping with strangers in Alaska, I ate vegan food out of dumpsters with anarchists, I even let some random modeling agency take pictures of me (that one was genuinely a terrible idea). Bit by bit, I discovered who I really was.

But it wasn't until I started unpacking my own story that I fully understood what I was meant to create. Stories are how humans create meaning, so to understand the meaning of my life, I had to understand my story. As I dug in, I found two things: building things and being in community. That long exploration eventually led to creating NationBuilder, the infrastructure for leaders to build thriving communities so that everyone has the freedom and opportunity to create what they are meant to create.

Understanding your story is not easy, and it's nearly impossible without talking to others about it—sit down with a friend and start sharing all the crazy stories of your lives with each other. You'll be able to help them see things they never saw, and they will do the same for you. Frequently we don't appreciate the thing we are exceptional at, because it comes so easily to us. Other people can see that in you, while you just take it for granted. Embrace it, master it, and contribute it to the world.

And then make it bigger. As big as you can imagine. Bigger than you could ever do by yourself. Because you don't have to do it by yourself anymore. You can build a community, you can raise money, you can harness the gifts and talents of strangers you've never even met, because they believe in your story, your vision, you. You can *lead*.

Every person who makes this leap, this commitment to fulfilling their purpose, will take us all one step closer to unlocking the potential of a connected humanity. One step closer to becoming the God we want to be.

What would the world look like if every one of us were doing what we are meant to do? If we were each creating what we are meant to create?

I have no idea, but I can't wait to find out.

ACKNOWLEDGMENTS

Writing this book was very hard. Partly because books are hard to write, but also because I'm very shy and far more comfortable envisioning the future than remembering the past. So I needed a lot of help. I am especially grateful to:

Jesse Coleman, for replacing parentheses with em dashes (among other editing magic), while booting up an entire book-publishing operation. Georgia Cool, for replacing em dashes with colons: she is a wonderful copy editor. Jonathan Lippincott, for designing the book and cover.

Robert Greenwald, for teaching me the power of stories. Kerry Candaele, for helping me appreciate the potential of my own story.

Micah Sifry, for putting me onstage to tell that story. Felicia Horowitz and Bob Endres for offering their homes as writing retreats. Jesse Haff, Laura Harris, and Andrew Rasiej, for very helpful feedback on an early draft. Seth Godin and Jessey White-Cinis, who, when I asked them both what the icon of the internet religion should be, each independently came up with **#** . . . surely a sign from God.

Ramin Bastani, my dearest friend, for his never-ending encouragement and support for this book. Ben Horowitz, for writing the foreword even after he read the book and found out how "witheringly judgmental" I was as a teenager. The NationBuilder community, both staff and alumni, who carried me through all of this and who make it possible for me to create what I am meant to create, every day.

My dad, for spending hours telling me stories about my early life and answering all my random text messages about obscure details. Maggie Gilliam, for detailed blogging of everything related to my lung transplant. Kristen Gilliam, for fearlessly letting me share her story, as it had such an impact on me. And my mom, Kathy Gilliam, who asked me to write this book nineteen years ago.

And finally, Lea Endres, the most extraordinary and selfless leader I will ever know. She didn't just write this book with me, she wrote the last five years of my life with me, helping me become the leader I need to be.